Medical Abbreviations

and other interpretive tools

Medical Abbreviations

and other interpretive tools

Compiled by

Jeevan Hingorani
of Gray's Inn, Barrister-at-law

Neville Sarony QC SC
of Gray's Inn

David Kan
Solicitor

With illustrations by Graeme Mackay
of Gray's Inn, Barrister-at-law

Infocus Communications

Published by Infocus Communications
Hong Kong
www.infocus.com.hk

Copyright © 2009 Jeevan Hingorani and Neville Sarony
Illustrations © 2009 Graeme Mackay

ISBN 978-988-99937-2-6

Printed in Hong Kong by Green Legend Production

Disclaimer
Although the authors and editors of this book have made every effort to ensure that the
information is accurate, the authors, editors and publisher do not accept responsibility
and hereby disclaim any liability to any party for any loss or damage arising from errors,
omissions or misleading information.

Contents

Foreword

Sir Denys Roberts, former Chief Justice, wrote the Foreword to Valerie Ann Penlington's *Law in Hong Kong* (1978), reputedly the first treatise on the subject, and derided that lawyers flourish in obscurity but not in total darkness. His Lordship confidently predicted that the book would be widely welcomed by solicitors, barristers, students, laymen, the casual reader and members of the Judiciary. May I also predict with confidence that *Medical Abbreviations* will be welcomed by a like audience and beyond as an original effort to deciphering doctors' enigmatic notes here in Hong Kong.

We are brought up to heed the advice of doctors, and it is important to understand exactly what they meant to say. It was anecdotal in South Australia that a juryman asked for discharge from the service and explained that the doctor had told him his wife was to be conceived any moment and he ought to be with her, whereby the judge retorted that the doctor must have meant confined, as opposed to conceived, but in any case, his presence would be desirable.

But seriously, for those of us who have the occasion to read doctors' notes and are laymen in medicine, we must have been bewildered by signs and abbreviations, the meaning of which may not be all too apparent. It has become more settled practice in personal-injuries litigation that medical experts are not called upon to give evidence orally unless the difference of opinion cannot be resolved on materials before the court. Very often, the treating doctors' notes provide the crux in resolving the diametric stances of parties' experts. This work will no doubt be of great assistance as a handy reference in court without troubling the doctors. Further, the section on Prefixes and Suffixes is useful in understanding the roots of the medical terms of Greek or Latin origin.

May I commend the ingenuity, industry and learning of Neville, Jeevan and David in the conception and production of this book. The caricatures of Graeme Mackay treated an otherwise dreary subject with a dosage of light-heartedness. I venture to say that the addition of meanings in Chinese in a sequel to the work will be eagerly awaited. As to the doctors' handwriting... perhaps greater endeavour of dexterity beckons.

Barnabas Fung
Judge of the High Court

Hong Kong 2009

Editors' note

Poring over barely decipherable hospital records and GP notes whilst considering claims in personal injuries, clinical negligence and professional inquiries, we encountered the additional hurdle of interpreting medical abbreviations and hieroglyphics, even though JH read medicine for four years before turning to the law. That led to the idea of compiling a hand-held lexicon for the enlightenment not only of ourselves but of all those who need to have ready reference to and understand what, to all intents and appearances, is a secret code, be they lawyers, judges or, may we suggest, even medical students. Whereas the vast bulk of these abbreviations are largely international, there are local variants; we hope that each user of our little vade mecum will notify the editors so that we may add in examples that we missed out. JH also added chapters on Signs and Symbols, Prefixes and Suffixes of medical words, Ranges of Motion and Common Orthopaedic, Neurological and Other Tests to give the work greater utility.

We are indebted to Dr David Kan for having reviewed all the entries and made his own invaluable and, dare we say, sometimes tongue-in-cheek British contributions. The colourful illustrations by Graeme are intended to cast a less serious light on a work which we hope will prove as useful to others as it has been to us.

Last, but by no means least, we are also greatly indebted to The Honourable Mr Justice Fung for his early recognition of the benefits of the book; inter alia, in avoiding the need to call medical experts on matters that should not require their absence from more humanitarian duties; and for his foresight in suggesting a sequel to incorporate meanings in Chinese, a suggestion which we intend to pursue promptly.

JH
NS

Hong Kong 2009

A

A	Abnormal / Abortion / Anterior / Attendance / not / without / Adenine or Adenosine
ā	Before
A$_2$	Aortic Second Sound
A&D	Admission and Discharge
A&E	Accident and Emergency
A&O	Alert and Oriented
A&P	Auscultation and Percussion
A&R	Advised and Released
A&W	Alive and Well
ABC	Aspiration Biopsy Cytology
A/V	Anteverted
AA	Alleged Assault / Aortic Aneurysm / Aplastic Anaemia
Aa	of each
aa	so much of each
AAA	Abdominal Aortic Aneurysm / Acute Anxiety Attack
aato	activity as tolerated
AAW	Alive and Well
AB	Apex Beat / Blood Group AB
Abd	Abduction
Abdo	Abdomen
ABG	Arterial Blood Gas Analysis
Abx	Antibiotics
Abn	Abnormal
ABPA	Allergic Bronchopulmonary Aspergillus
AC	Atrial Contraction / Acromioclavicular / Air-Conditioning / Alternating Current / Anodal Closure / Aortic Closure
Ac	Before meals / Actinium
ac	Before Meals

ac & cl	acetest and clinitest
ACD	Acid Citrate Dextrose
ACE	Angiotension Converting Enzyme
ACEI	Angiotension Converting Enzyme Inhibitor
A Ch	Acetylcholine
AChE	Acetylcholinesterase
ACLS	Advanced Cardiac Life Support
ACPS	Acrocephalopolysyndactyly
ACT	Activated Clotting Time
ACTH	Adrenocorticotropic Hormone
AcG	Accelerator Globulin (coagulation factor V)
AD	Admission and Discharge / Admitting Diagnosis / Afer Discharge / Alternating Days / Alzheimer's Disease / Anxiety Disease / Right Ear
ad	to
ADA	Adenosine Deaminase
ADCC	Antibody-Dependent Cell-mediated Cytotoxicity
ADD	Attention Deficit Disorder
Add	Adduction
ADE	Acute Disseminated Encephalomyelitis
ADH	Antidiuretic Hormone / Alcohol Dehydrogenase
ADHD	Attention-Deficit Hyperactivity Disorder
ADL	Activities of Daily Living
ADM	Acquired Dermal Melanocystosis
adm	Admission
ADP	Adenosine Diphosphate
AE	Accident and Emergency / Air

	Embolism / Air Entry / Equal		Lymphadenopathy with Dysproteinemia
AET	Zidovudine	**AIP**	Acute Intermittent Porphyria
AEQ	Diaziquone	**Aj**	Ankle jerk
AF	Artificial Feeding / Atrial Fibrillation	**AK**	Above Knee / Artificial Kidney
AFB	Acid Fast Bacillus	**AKA**	Above Knee Amputation / Also Known
AFP	Alfa Foeto Protein		As
AFX	Atypical Fibroxanthoma	**AL**	Acute Leukaemia
AG	Albumin : Globulin Ratio / Atrial	**Alb**	Albumin
	Gallop	**ALG**	Antilymphocyte Globulin
AGT	Antiglobulin Test	**ALL**	Acute Lymphoblastic Leukemia
Ag	Silver	**ALS**	Amyotrophic Lateral Sclerosis /
AH	Arterial Hypertension / Auditory		Antilymphocyte Serum
	Hallucination	**Alte die**	Alternative days
AHF	Anti-Hemophilic Factor	**Alte nocte**	Alternative nights
AHG	Anti-Hemophilic Globulin	**Amn**	Amnion
AHR	Artificial Hip Replacement	**AMA**	Against Medical Advice
AI	Accidental Injury / Aortic Insufficiency	**AML**	Acute Myelogenous Leukemia
	/ Artificial Insemination	**amb**	ambulate / walk
AID	Artificial Donor Insemination	**AMI**	Acute Myocardial Infarction
AIDS	Acquired-Immune Deficiency	**AMP**	Adenosine Monophosphate
	Syndrome	**amp**	amputate
AIH	Artificial Heterologous Insemination	**amt**	Amount
AILD	Angioimmunoblastic	**An**	Anode

AE
Accident and Emergency

11

ana	of each	**Arg**	Arginine
ANC	Ante-Natal Clinic	**ART**	Automated Reagin Test
ANF	Antinuclear factor	**AS**	Ankylosing Spondylitis / Aortic
ANP	Atrial Natriuretic Peptide		Stenosis / Arteriosclerosis
ANS	Autonomic Nervous System	**ASA**	Aspirin / Acetylsalicylic Acid
ant	anterior	**as tol**	as tolerated
ANUG	Acute Necrotizing Ulceratlve	**ASCVD**	Arteriosclerotic Cardiovascular
	Gingivitus		Disease
AO	Abdominal Aorta / Acid Output / Airway	**ASD**	Atrial Septal Defect
	Obstruction	**ASF**	Anterior Spinal Fusion
Ao	Aorta	**ASH**	Asymmetrical Septal Hypertrophy
AP	Action Potential / Angina Pectoris	**ASHD**	Arteriosclerotic Heart Disease
	/ Anterior Pituitary (gland) /	**Asn**	Asparagine
	Anteroposterior / Action Potential	**Aso**	Arteriosclerosis obliterans
Ap	Apex / Apical	**Asp**	Aspartic Acid
ap	before dinner	**AST**	Aspartate Aminotransferase
APC	Atrial Premature Complex / Activated	**Astig**	Astigmatism
	Protein C	**AT**	Achilles Tendon / Atrial Tachycardia
APE	Acute Pulmonary Oedema / Anterior	**ATL**	Adult T-Cell Leukemia / Lymphoma
	Pituitary Extract	**ATN**	Acute Tubular Necrosis
APH	Antepartum Haemorrhage	**ATNR**	Asymmetrical Tonic Neck Reflex
APPT	Activated Partial Prothrombin Time	**ATP**	Adenosine Triphosphate
APUD	Amine Precursor Uptake and	**AUL**	Acute Undifferentiated Leukemia
	Decarboxylation	**Au**	Both Ears / Both Ears Together
AQ/Aq	Achievement Quotient	**Ausc**	Auscultation
Aq	Aqueous	**AV**	Aortic Valve / Artificial Ventilation /
aq	aqueous		Assisted Ventilation / Arteriovenous
AR	Apical-Radial / At Risk / Atrial Rate /	**Av**	Average / Avoirdupois
	Alarm Reaction / Aortic Regurgitation /	**AVB**	Atrioventricular Block
	Artificial Respiration	**AVM**	Arteriovenous Malformation
Ar	Argon	**AVN**	Avascular Necrosis / Atrioventricular
ARDS	Acute Respiratory Distress Syndrome		Node
ARF	Acute Renal Failure	**AVR**	Atrial Valve Replacement
AROM	Artificial Rupture of Membranes	**AVRT**	Atrioventricular Reciprocating
ART	Automated Reagin Test		Tachycardia
Art	Artery	**AVS**	Aortic Valve Stenosis
ara-A	Adenine Arabinoside	**Ax**	Axillary
ara-C	cytarabine	**ax**	axillary, axial
ARC	AIDS-Related Complex / Anomalous	**AXR**	Abdominal X-Ray
	Retinal Correspondence		

B

b	born / base	**Bili**	Bilirubin
BA	Brachial Artery / Bronchial Asthma	**BK**	Below the Knee
Ba	Barium	**BKA**	Below Knee Amputation
BAL	Blood Alcohol Level / Dimercaprol	**BKV**	BK Virus
Ba M	Barium Meal	**bl**	blood
BaB	Babinski's Sign	**BL**	Blood Level / Blood Loss
BaE	Barium Enema	**bl cult.**	blood culture
Barb	Barbiturates	**bl wk**	blood work
BAV	Bicuspid Aortic Value	**BL-GAS**	Blood Gases
BB	Baby Boy / Breast Biopsy	**BLS**	Basic Life Support
BBa	Born Before Arrival	**Bm**	Bone Marrow / Body Mass
BBB	Blood Brain Barrier / Bundle Branch Block	**BM**	Bowel Movement
		BMH	Bowel Movement Heard
BBBB	Bilateral Bundle Branch Block	**BMI**	Body Mass Index
BBx	Breast Biopsy	**BMR**	Basal Metabolic Rate
BC	Blood Count / Blood Culture		
BCC	Basal Cell Carcinoma		
BCDF	B Cell Differentiation Factors		
BCG	Bacille Calmette-Guerin		
BCNU	Carmustine		
BD	Birth Date / Birth Defect / Borderline Dull / Brain Damage / Twice a day		
bdr	twice a day		
BE	Bacterial Endocarditis / Barium Enema		
bf	boyfriend		
BF	Body Fat		
BG	Blood Glucose		
BHA	Butylated hydroxyanisole		
BHT	Butylated Hydroxytoluene		
BI	Body Injury / Bone Injury / Brain Injury		
bid	twice a day		

BS
Babinski's Sign

BMT	Bone Marrow Transplantation		Sugar / Bowel Sounds / Breath Sounds
BNO	Bowels Not Open / Bladder Neck Obstruction	**BS+**	Bowel Sound Audible or Present
		BSB	Bedside Bag
BO	Bowels Open	**BSF**	B Lymphocyte Stimulatory factor
BOW	Bag of Waters	**bt**	bedtime
BP	Birth Place / Blood Pressure	**BT**	Blood Transfusion / Blood Type / Body
BPIG	Bacterial Polysaccharide Immune Globulin		Temperature / Brain Tumour / Breast Tumour
bp	base pair	**BU**	Blood Urea
bpm	beats per minute	**BUN**	Blood, Urea, Nitrogen
Bq	Becquerel	**BV**	Blood Vessel
br	breath	**BVAD**	Biventricular Assist Device
BR	Bed Rest / Breathing Rate	**BVM**	Bag Valve Mask
BRM	Biological Response Modifier	**BW**	Birth Weight / Body Weight
BS	Babinski's Sign / Before Sleep / Blood	**Bx**	Biopsy

C

C	Calorie / Celsius / Centigrade	**C VIII**	Eighth Cranial Nerve (Vestibulocochlear)
c	concentration / culture	**C IX**	Ninth Cranial Nerve (Glossopharyngeal)
c̄	with	**C X**	Tenth Cranial Nerve (Vagus)
C&E	Consultation and Examination	**C XI**	Eleventh Cranial Nerve (Accessory)
C&H	Coarse and Harsh (Breathing)	**C XII**	Twelfth Cranial Nerve (Hypoglossal)
C&R	Cardiac and Respiratory	**C1**	First Cervical Vertebra
C&S	Culture and Sensitivity	**C2**	Second Cervical Vertebra , and so on
C&T	Colour and Temperature	**C₁INH**	C1 Inhibitor
C I	First Cranial Nerve (Olfactory)	**C₃NeF**	C3 Nephritic Factor
C II	Second Cranial Nerve (Optic)	**CD**	Cardiac Dysrhythmia / Caesarian
C III	Third Cranial Nerve (Occulomotor)		Delivery / Common Duct / Conduction
C IV	Fourth Cranial Nerve (Trochlear)		Disorder / Current Diagnosis / Cadaveric
C V	Fifth Cranial Nerve (Trigeminal)		Donor / Curative Dose / Cluster
C VI	Sixth Cranial Nerve (Abducens)		Designation
C VII	Seventh Cranial Nerve (Facial)	**CD₅₀**	Median Curative Dose

C/E	Clinical Examination
C/I	Clinical Investigation
c/o	complaining of / current complaint
c/s	Caesarian Section
C/ST	Contraction Stress Test
Ca	Calcium
CA	Cancer / Cardiac Arrest / Carotid Artery / Coronary Artery
CAA	Chronic Aplastic Anaemia
CAB	Coronary Artery Bypass
CABG	Coronary Artery Bypass Graft Surgery
CABS	Coronary Bypass Surgery
CAD	Coronary Artery Disease
CAE	Coronary Artery Embolism
CAF	Continuous Atrial Fibrillation
CAH	Chronic Active Hepatitis
Cal	Calorie
CAMP	Cyclic Adenosine Monophosphate
CAP	Prostate Cancer
CAPD	Continuous Ambulatory Peritoneal Dialysis
caps	capsules
CAR	Computer Assisted Radiology
Carb	Carbohydrate / Carbonate
Cas	Casualty
CAT	Computed Axial Tomography
Cat	Cataract
Cath	Catheter
cav	cavity
CB	Ceased Breathing
CBC	Complete Blood Count
CBD	Common Bile Duct
CBP	Calcium Binding Protein / Combined Blood Picture
Cbl	Cobalamin
CC	Chief Complaint
CCU	Coronary Care unit
CCNU	Lomustine
CD	Caesarian Delivery / Common Duct / Crohn's Disease / Current Diagnosis

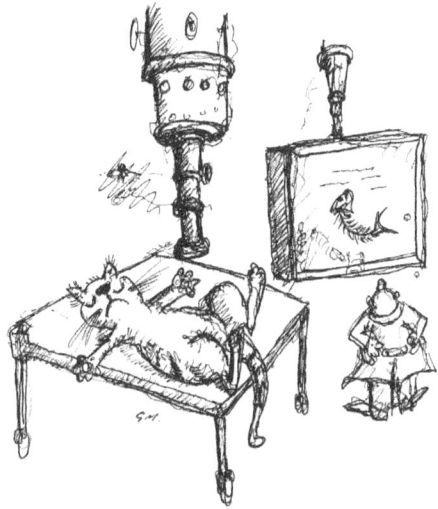

CAT
Computed Axial Tomography

CDH	Congenital Dislocation of Hip
ce-ca	cervical cancer
CEA	Carcinoembrionic Antigen
CEP	Congenital Erythropoietic Porphyria
CESD	Cholesteryl Ester Storage Disease
CFT	Cardiac Function Tests / Compliment Fixation Test
CGS	Centimetre-Gram-Second System
CGU	Chronic Gastric Ulcer
cGy	Centrigray
CH	Chronic Hepatitis / Chronic Hypertension
Ch	Chest
CHB	Complete Heart Block
CHD	Common Hepatic Duct / Congenital / Congestive / Coronary Heart Disease
CHF	Congestive Heart Failure
CHL	Crown-Heel Length
ChE	Cholinesterase
Chol	Cholesterol

CI	Cerebral Infarction / Chronic Infection / Clinical Impression / Clinical Investigation / Cardiac Index / Colour Index
Ci	Curie
CK	Creatine Kinase
CLD	Chronic Lung Disease
CLL	Chronic Lymphocytic Leukaemia
CIN	measurement of Cervical cancer / Cervical Intraepithelial Neoplasia
CIS	Carcinoma in situ
cl	centalitre / clinical
Cl	Chloride / Chlorine / Clear
cl liq	clear liquid
cm	centimetre
CM	Cardiac Murmur / Caucasian Male
CMD	Cerebromuscular Degeneration
CMI	Cell-Mediated Immunity
CMT	Certified Medical Transcriptionist
CMV	Cytomegalovirus
Cm	Curium
cm/cm3	centimetre / cubic centimetre
CN	Cranial Nerve
CNS	Central Nervous System
CO	Cardiac Output / Carbon Monoxide / Casualty Officer / Complains of
CO$_2$	Carbon Dioxide
COAD	Chronic Obstructive Airway Disease
COPD	Chronic Obstructive Pulmonary Disease
COS	Chief of Service
Co	Cobalt
CoA	CoEnzyme A
CP	Cardiac Performance / Cerebral Palsy / Chest Pain / Chicken Pox / Chronic Pain / Clinical Pathology
CPD	Cephalo Parietal / Pelvic Disproportion
CPDD	Calcium Pyrophosphate Deposition Disease
CPD#	Compound Fracture
CPK	Creatine Phosphokinase
CPR	Cardiopulmonary Resuscitation

CPR
Cardiopulmonary Resuscitation

CPRS	Complex Regional Pain Syndrome
cpm	counts per minute
cps	cycles per second
CR	Cardiac Resuscitation / Closed Reduction / Computed Radiograph / Conditioned Reflex (response)
CRH	Corticotropin-Releasing Hormone
Cr	Chromium
Cr N	Cranial Nerve
cr nn	Cranial Nerves
CRC	Crown Rump Circumference
CRF	Chronic Renal Failure
Creps	Crepitations
CRL	Crown Rump Length
cRNA	complementary RNA
CS	Cerebrospinal / Cervical Spine / Caesarian Section / Cigarette Smoker / Close Supervision / Conscious Sedation / Conditioned Stimulus / Coronary Sinus
Cs	Case / Cesium
CSF	Cerebro Spinal Fluid
c-spine	cervical spine
CST	Culture and Sensitivity Test
CT	Chest Tube / Computer Axial Tomograph / Total Cholesterol

CTP	Cystidine Triphosphate	**CVP**	Central Venous Pressure
CTL	Cytotoxic T Lymphocytes	**CVS**	Cardiovascular Surgery / Cardiovascular
CTG	Cardiotocograph (Foetal Heart Monitor)		System / Chorionic Villus Sampling /
Cu	Copper		Current Vital Signs
CU	Cardiac Unit / Cause Unknown	**CVU**	Cardiovascular Unit
CV	Central Venous / Fifth Cranial Nerve	**CW**	Children's Ward
CVA	Cerebral Vascular Accident / Stroke	**Cx**	Cancel / Cervix / Complaint / Complication
CVI	Cortical Visual Impairment	**CXR**	Chest X-ray
CVID	Common Variable Immunodeficiency	**Cysto**	Cystography

D

D	Date / Daughter / Day / Deceased /		/ Drug Addict
	Diagnosis / Dorsal / Density / Dose /	**da**	daughter
	Duration	**DAC**	Decitabine
d	daily	**DAF**	Decay Accelerating Factor
D1-D12	Dorsal Vertebrae	**DAMA**	Discharged Against Medical Advice
D&C	Dilatation and Curettage	**DAT**	Diet As Tolerated
D/C	Discharged	**DB**	Date of Birth / Diabetic / Diabetes
D_5D_{20}	Dextrose Solution	**Db**	Diabetes / Diabetic
D&V	Diarrhoea and Vomiting	**DBA**	Dead Before Arrival
D/O	Dissolved Oxygen	**Dbili**	Direct Bilirubin
D/W	Discussed with / Dextrose Water	**DC**	Descending Colon / Dilatation and
D5/NS	Dextrose 5% / Normal Saline (example)		Curettage / Discontinue / Direct Current
DA	Descending Aorta / Digital Angiography	**dc**	decrease / discontinue

DAMA
Discharged Against Medical Advice

DCIS	Ductal Carcinoma In Situ		Degeneration
DD	Discharge Diagnosis / Dangerous Drug	**DRUJ**	Distal Radio-Ulnar Joint
	/ Degenerative Disease / Differential	**DS**	Dead Space / Delayed Sensitivity /
	Diagnosis / Digestive Disorder		Dextrose Solution / Discharge Summary
DDT	Dichloro-Diphenyl-Trichloroethane		/ Down Syndrome
Dec'd	Deceased	**DSA**	Digital Subtraction Arteriogram
DES	Diethylstilbestrol	**DT**	Discharge Tomorrow
DET	Diethyltryptamine	**DTaP**	Diphtheria and Tetanus Toxoids and
DH	Dominant Hand / Drug History		Acellular Pertussis Vaccine
DI	Date of Injury / Diabetes Insipidus	**DTP**	Diphtheria and Tetanus Toxoids and
DIC	Diffuse Intravascular Coagulation /		Pertussis Vaccine
	Disseminated Intravascular Coagulation	**DTR**	Deep Tendon Reflexes
DL	Diagnostic Laparoscopy / Diagnostic	**DTs**	Delirium Tremens
	Laparotomy / Direct Laryngoscopy	**DU**	Duodenal Ulcer
dl	decilitre	**DVT**	Deep Vein Thrombosis
DLE	Discoid Lupus Erythematosus	**DW**	Doing Well / Down / Discuss with
DM	Degenerative Myelopathy / Diabetes	**Dx**	Diagnosis
	Mellitus / Diastolic Murmur	**DX**	Diagnosis
dm	dorso-medial	**Dz**	Disease
DMFO	Eflornithine		
DMSO	Dimethyl Sulfoxide		
DMT	Dimethyltryptamide		
DN	Do Not		
DNA	Did Not Attend		
DNC	Dilatation and Curettage		
DNR	Do Not Resuscitate		
DNS	Deviated Nasal Septum		
DO	Doctor's Orders / Drugs Only / Drug		
	Overdose		
do	ditto		
DO$_2$	Oxygen Delivery		
DOA	Date of Admission / Date of Arrival /		
	Dead on Arrival / Dead on Admission /		
	Department of Anesthesia		
DOB	Date of Birth		
DP	Diastolic Pressure / Distal Phalanx		
DPT	Diphtheria-Pertussis-Tetanus		
Dysp	Whooping Cough, Tetanus		
	Dyspnoea		
DR	Delivery Room / Reaction of		

DNS
Deviated Nasal Septum

E

E&A	Evaluate and Advise	**EG**	External Genitalia
E&M	Evaluation and Management	**EHBA**	Extrahepatic Biliary Atresia
E&R	Equal and Reactive	**EKY**	Electrokymography
E Coli	Escherichia Coli	**ELISA**	Enzyme-linked Immuno-Sorbent Assay
EAC	Erythrocyte Antibody Complement	**elb**	elbow
	(used in studies of complement)	**EM**	Electron Micrograph / Electron
EAM	External Auditory Meatus		Microscope
ea	each	**Em**	Emmetropia
EBV	Epstein-Barr Virus	**EMF**	Electromotive Force
	Electrocardiogram/Elective Caesarian /	**EMG**	Electromyelogram
EC	Enteric Coated	**EMU**	Early Morning Urine Specimen
ECABS	Emergency Coronary Artery Bypass	**EN**	Enrolled Nurse
	Surgery	**End**	Endoscopy
ECF-A	Eosinophil Chemotactic Factor of	**ENG**	Electronystagmography
	Anaphylaxis	**ENT**	Ear, Nose and Throat
ECG	Electrocardiogram	**EOG**	Electro-Olfactogram
ECMO	Extracorporeal Membrane	**EP**	Epilepsy / Evoked Potential
	Oxygenation	**EPA**	Eicosapentaenoic Acid
Echo	Echocardiography	**EPAN**	Epidural Anaesthesia
ECS	Elective Caesarian Section	**EPAP**	Expiratory Positive Airway Pressure
ECT	Electroconvulsive Therapy	**EPG**	Early Prima Gravida
ED	Effective Dose / Emotionally Disturbed	**ER**	Endoplasmic Reticulum / Oestrogen
ED$_{50}$	Median Effective Dose		Receptor / Emergency Room
EDC	Estimated Date of Conception /	**ERBF**	Effective Renal Blood Flow
	Estimated Date of Confinement	**ERCP**	Endoscopic Retrograde Cholangio-
EDD	Estimated Date of Delivery / Estimated		Pancreatography
	Discharge Date / Estimated Due Date	**ERP**	Endocardial Resection Procedure
EDRF	Endothelial-Derived Relaxant Factor	**ERPF**	Effective Renal Plasma Flow
EDTA	Ethylendeiamine Tetraacetic Acid	**ESR**	Erythrocyte Sedimentation Rate
EDV	End-Diastolic Volume	**ERV**	Expiratory Reserve Volume
EEE	Eastern Equine Encephalomyelitis	**ESRD**	End Stage Renal Disease
EEG	Electroencephalography	**ESRF**	End Stage Renal Failure
EENT	Eye-Ear-Nose-Throat	**EST**	Electroshock Therapy

ESV	End-Systolic Volume	**ET Tube**	Endotracheal Tube
ext	extract	**ETT**	Endotracheal Tube
ET-NANB	Enterically Transmitted Non-A, Non-B	**EUA**	Examination Under Anaesthetic
	Hepatitis	**EvD**	Extra ventricular Drainage

F

F	Fahrenheit / Father / Female /	**FBG**	Fasting Blood Glucose
	Frequency / Fluorine	**FBI**	Fasting Blood Insulin
F1	First Filial Generation	**FBM**	Fresh Bone Marrow
F2	Second Filial Generation	**FBP**	Femoral Blood Pressure
5-FU	Fluorouracil	**FBS**	Foetal Blood Sample / Foetal Blood
F^U	Fingers above Umbilicus		Sampling
F Cath	Foley's Catheter	**FBV**	Foetal Blood Volume
F&D	Fixed and Dilated	**FC**	Foley's Catheter / Functional Capacity
F&R	Force and Rhythm (of pulse)	**FCC**	Fracture Complete and Comminuted
F$_1$O$_2$	Forced Inspiratory Oxygen / Oxygen	**FCD**	Fibrocystic Dysplasia
	Fraction	**FCE**	Functional Capacity Evaluation
FA	Fasting for 72 hours / Femoral Artery	**FCh**	Free Cholesterol
	/ Foetal Age / Foetal Artery / First	**FCM**	Flow Cytometry
	Admission / Food Allergy / Fully Awake /	**FCS**	Forceps
	Functional Assessment	**FCx**	Frontal Cortex
fac	factor	**FD**	Foetal Distress
FAD	Flavin Aderine Dinucleotide	**fdg**	feeding
FAH	Family History	**FDIU**	Foetal Death In Utero
fam	family	**Fe**	Female / Iron
fam hist	family history	**Fe Def**	Iron Deficiency
FB	Foreign Body	**Feb**	Febrile
fb	fibre	**FeBe**	Feeling Better
FBA	Foetal Blood Analysis	**febr**	febrile
FBC	Female Breast Carcinoma / Foetal Brain	**FEC**	Forced Expiratory Capacity
	Cells / Full Blood Count	**FED**	Functional Erectile Dysfunction
FBE	Full Blood Examination	**FEDI**	Foetal Distress
FBF	Femoral Blood Flow	**FEF**	Forced Expiratory Flow

FEFX	Femoral Fracture
FEM	Fast Eye Movement
fem	female / femoral / femur
FEO	For Evaluation Of
FEUO	For External Use Only
FEV	Forced Expiratory Volume
fev	Fever
FEW	Foetal Weight
FEWKS	Few Weeks
FFA	Free Fatty Acids
FFD	Fat Free Diet
FFF	Fast Freeze Fixation
FFI	Free From Infection
FFP	Fresh Frozen Plasma
FFROM	Full and Free Range of Motion
FFS	Fat Free Solids
FGLU	Fasting Glucose
FGT	Female Genital Tract
FGX	Fluid Gas Exchange
FH	Family History / Foetal Head / Foetal Heart

FLR
Funny Looking Rash

FH-	Family History Negative	**FHT**	Foetal Heart / Foetal Heart Tracing
FH+	Family History Positive	**FHx**	Family History
FHB	Foetal Heart Beat / Fulminant Hepatitis B	**Fib**	Fibre / Fibrillation / Fibrosis / Fibula
FHb	Free Haemoglobin	**Fibrill**	Fibrillation
FHBC	Family History of Breast Cancer	**FIC**	Forced Inspiratory Capacity
FHD	Family History of Diabetes	**FICU**	Foetal Intensive Care Unit
FHH	Foetal Heart Heard	**FIGLU**	Formiminoglutamic Acid
FHHR	Foetal Heart Heard and Regular	**FIUO**	For Internal Use Only
FHL	Functional Hearing Loss	**FIV**	Fertilisation In Vitro / Forced Inspiratory Volume
FHMI	Family History of Mental Illness		
FHN	Femoral Head and Neck / Negative Family History	**FKD**	Family History of Kidney Disease
		FKE	Full Knee Extension
FHNH	Foetal Heart Not Heard	**FL**	Femur Length / Foetal Length / Fluid
FHP	Family History Positive	**fl**	fluid
FHR	Foetal Heart Rate	**fl up**	follow up
FHRM	Foetal Heart Rate Monitoring	**fld**	fluid
FHS	Foetal Heart Sounds / Follicle Stimulating Hormone / Fresh Human Serum	**fld.rest.**	fluid restriction
		FLE	Fontal Lobe Epilepsy
		flex	flexion

FLGI	Fluids Given	**FSH/RH**	Follicle-Stimulating Hormone-Releasing
FLR	Funny Looking Rash		Hormone
FM	Foetal Movement	**FSP**	Finger Systolic Pressure
FMF	Foetal Movements Felt	**FST**	For Some Time
FMH	Family Medical History	**FT**	Feeding Tube / Full Term
FMN	Flavin Mononucleotide	**Ft**	Feet / Foot
Fn	Function	**FTBDT**	Felt To Be Due To
FNAB	Fine Needle Aspiration Biopsy	**FTBN**	Found To Be Normal
FNB	Fine Needle Biopsy	**FTD**	Failure To Descend
FNF	Femoral Neck Fracture	**FTHR**	Foetal Heart Rate
FNI	Fine Needle Injection	**FTKA**	Failed To Keep Appointment
FO	Foreign Object	**FTLB**	Full Term Live Birth
FoB	Front of Bed	**FTNB**	Full Term Newborn
FoBY	Followed By	**FTND**	Full Term Normal Delivery
FOC	Family History of Ovarian Cancer	**FTP**	Failure To Progress
FoFU	For Follow Up	**FTR**	For The Record / For This Reason
FooB	Fell Out Of Bed	**FTRE**	Failed To Reveal
For:	Investigations to be Conducted	**FTRT**	Failed To Respond To
FoUP	Follow Up	**FTSS**	Frozen Tissue Smears
Fr	Frequency	**FTT**	Failure To Thrive
FR	Full Rate	**FTVD**	Full Term Vaginal Delivery
Frac	Fracture	**FU**	Fingers Below Umbilicus / Follow Up
FrBB	Fracture of Both Bones	**FUDR**	Floxuridine
FRC	Functional Residual Capacity /	**FUE**	Fever of Unknown Aetiology
	Functional Residual Lung Capacity	**FUINF**	Fully Informed
FRF	Functional Renal Failure	**FUMA**	Further Management
FRJM	Full Range Joint Movement	**FUN**	Follow Up Note
FROM	Full Range of Motion	**FUO**	Fever Of Unknown Origin
FRT	Full Recovery Time	**FUOB**	Further Observation
FRTL	Frontal	**FUOR**	Fully Oriented
Frx	Fracture	**FUR**	Follow Up Report / Further
FSA	Frozen Section Analysis	**FUST**	Full Strength
FSD	Fracture Simple and Depressed	**FVBF**	Femoral Venous Blood Flow
FSE	Foetal Scalp Electrode / Frozen Section	**FVC**	Forced Vital Capacity
	Examination	**FVE**	Forced Volume Expiration
FSF	Fibrin-Stabilizing Factor	**FW**	Few
FSH	Follicle Stimulating Hormone	**FWB**	Full Weight Bearing
FSH/	Follicle-Stimulating Hormone and	**FWD**	Forward
LH-RH	Luteinizing Hormone-Releasing	**Fx**	Fracture
	Hormone	**FxBB**	Fracture of Both Bones

FXCT	Fluorescent X-Ray Computed Tomography	**FXS**	Fracture
		FXSI	Fracture Site
FXDI	Fracture Dislocation	**FYI**	For Your Information
Fx-dis	Fracture dislocation	**FYW**	Fat Young Woman

G

G	Glucose / Good / Gravida / Gauss	**GBD**	Gall Bladder Disease
g	gram	**GC**	Gas Chromatography / General Circulation / General Condition
G-	Gram Negative		
G&D	Growth and Development	**GCC**	Giant Cell Carcinoma
G&W	Glycerin and Water	**GCS**	General Condition Stable / Glasgow Coma Scale
G/C	General Condition		
G+	Gram Positive	**GCSF**	Granulocyte Colony-Stimulating Factor
G±	Growth Inhibiting / Primagravida	**GCT**	Giant Cell Tumour (of bone)
G1 Po	Gravida 1 Post Operative	**GCV**	Great Cardiac Vein
G6PD	An Enzyme In Blood / Glucose-6-Phosphate Dehyolrogenase	**GCY**	Gastroscopy
		Gd	Gadolinium (chemical symbol)
GA	General Anaesthesia / General Anaesthetic / General Appearance / Gestational Age	**GD HE**	Good Health
		GE	Gastroenteritis / General Examination
Ga	Gallium (chemical symbol)		
GABA	X-Aminobutyric Acid		
GAD	Generalized Anxiety Disease		
GA End	General Anaesthesia with Endotracheal Intubation		
GACA	Gastric Cancer		
GALT	Gnt-Associated Lymphoid Tissue		
Gang	Gangrene		
GAUL	Gastric Ulcer		
GB	Gall Bladder		
GB CA	Gall Bladder Cancer		

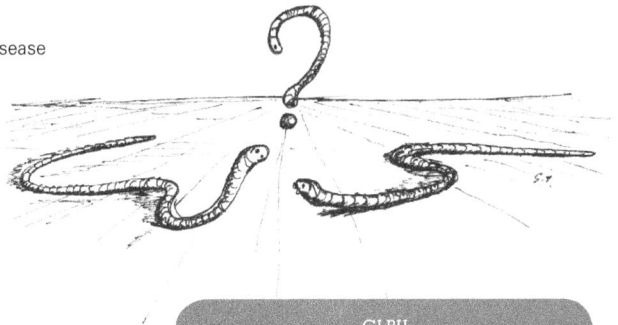

GLBU
Gay, Lesbian, Bisexual, Unsure

Ge	Germanium (chemical symbol)		Stimulating Factor
GER	Gastro-Oesophageal Reflux	gm	gram
GERD	Gastro-Oesophageal Reflux Disease	GM+	Gram Positive
Gest	Gestation	GM-ve	Gram Negative
Gev/	Gigaelectron Volt, One Billion (10 9)	GN	Glomerulonephritis
GevGev	Electron Volts	Gn-RH	Gonadotropin-Releasing Hormone
gf	girlfriend	GNB	Gram Negative Bacillus
GFAP	Glial Fibrillary Acidic Protein	GnPn	Gravida n. Parity n.
GFR	Glomerular Filtration Rate	GNP	Glomerulonephritis
GGT	Gamma Glutamyl Transferase	GO CO	Good Condition
GH	Good Health / Growth Hormone	GOAP	Good Appetite
GHD	Growth Hormone Deficiency	GOK	God Only Knows
GHG	General Health Good	GOT	Glumatic-Oxaloacetic Transaminase
GHIF	Growth Hormone Inhibiting Factor	GP	General Practitioner / General Paresis
GH-RH	Growth Hormone-Releasing Hormone	GPT	Glumatic-Pyruvic Transaminase
GI	Gastro Intestinal	Gp	General Practitioner, general paresis
GIB	Gastrointestinal Bleeding	gp	group
GIC	Gastrointestinal Cancer	GPB	Gram Positive Bacillus
GIT	Gastrointestinal Tract	GR	Good Recovery
GITT	Glucose Insulin Tolerance Test	GRH	Growth Hormone-Releasing Hormone
GI	Gland	GrN	Gram Negative
Glauc	Glaucoma	GRNR	Grossly Normal
GLBU	Gay, Lesbian, Bisexual, Unsure	GROM	Good Range of Motion
GLC	Gas Liquid Chromatography	GRSTR	Grip Strength
GLM	Good Looking Mother	GRUT	Gravid Uterus
GM	Gram / Grand Mal / Grey Matter	GS	Gall Stone
GMP	Guanosine Monophosphate	GSB	Graduated Spinal Block
GMCSF	Granulocyte-Macrophage Colony-	GSC	Gas Solid Chromatography

GT
Gastric Tube

GSE	Grips Strong and Equal	**Gtt**	Glucose Tolerance Test
GSH	Reduced Glutathione	**gtt.**	gutta (drops)
GSSG	Oxidized Glutathione	**Gtts**	Drops Per Minute
GT	Gastric Tube	**GTP**	Guanosine Triphosphate
gt.	gutta (drop)	**GU**	Genito-Urinary / Gastric Ulcer
GTB	Gastrointestinal Tract Bleeding	**GUT**	Genito-Urinary Tract
GTCC	Generalised Tonic-Clonic Convulsions	**GV**	Gas Ventilation
		GVHD	Graft-Versus-Host Disease
GTN	Gestational Trophoblastic Neoplasia	**GW**	Glycerin in Water
GTT	Glucose Tolerance Test	**GWB**	General Well Being

H

H	Heart / Height / Hernia / Hormone / Hour / Husband / Hydrogen / Hypothalamus		Vaccine
		HBE	His Bundle Electogram
		HBeAg	Hepatitis B E Antigen
H&E	Hematoxylin-eosin (stain)	**Hbg**	Haemoglobin
H&L	Heart and Lung	**HBOT**	Hyperbaric Oxygen Therapy
H&N	Head and Neck	**HBP**	High Blood Pressure
H&P	History and Physical Examination	**HBS**	Hepato-Biliary System / High Blood Sugar
H&T	Hospitalisation and Treatment		
h.s	at bedtime	**HBsAg**	Hepatitis B Surface Antigen
h/o	history of	**HBT**	Total Haemoglobin
H₂O	Water	**HBV**	Hepatitis B Virus
H₂O₂	Hydrogen Peroxide	**HC**	Head Circumference / Hepatitis C
HA	Headache / Hepatitis A	**HCC**	Hepatocellular Carcinoma / History of Current Complaint
HAART	Highly Active Anti Retroviral Therapy		
Haem	Haemotocrit / Haemotology	**HCG**	Human Chorionic Gonadotrophin
HAHO	Has a history of	**HCO₃**	Bicarbonate
HAI	Hospital Acquired Infection	**HCP**	Hereditary Coproporphyria
HAV	Hepatitis A Virus	**Hct**	Haematocrit
Hb	Haemoglobin	**HD**	Heart Disease / Hodgkin's Disease
HB	Heart Block / Hepatitis B	**Hd**	Head
HBCAg	Hepatitis B Core Antigen	**HDCV**	Human Diploid Cell Rabies Vaccine
HbCV	Haemophilus Influenzae B Conjugate	**HDL**	High Density Lipoprotein (Cholesterol)

HFD	High Forceps Delivery	**HOF**	Head of Femur
HELOS	Hearing Loss	**HP**	Hemiplegia
HEME	Haemorrhage	**Hp**	Hemiplegia
HEP	Hepatitis / Hepatoerythropoietic	**HPC**	History of Presenting Complaint
	Porphyria	**HPI**	History of Present Illness
HEP A	Hepatitis A	**HPL**	Human Placental Lactogen
HEP B	Hepatitis B	**HPLC**	High-Performance Liquid
HF	Head of Foetus / Heart Failure /		Chromatography
	Hageman Factor	**HPV**	Hepatic Portal Vein / Human Papilloma
hf	half / high frequency		Virus
HFHL	High Frequency Hearing Loss	**HR**	Heart Rate / Hospital Record
HFNI	Head, Face and Neck Injuries	**HRCT**	High-Resolution Computed Tomography
hg	haemoglobin	**HRF**	Histamine-Releasing Factor /
Hg	Mercury (chemical symbol)		Homologous Restriction Factor
Hgb	Haemoglobin	**HRM**	Heart Rate Monitor
Hg-F	Foetal Haemoglobin	**HRT**	Hormone Replacement Therapy
HGH, hGH	Human (Pituitary) Growth Hormone	**HS**	At Bedtime / Half Strength
hgt	Height	**hs**	at bedtime / history
HHD	Hypertensive Heart Disease	**HSA**	Human Serum Albumin
HHH	He Has Had	**HSAN**	Hereditary Sensory and Autonomic
HI	Head Injury		Neuropathy
HICH	High Cholesterol	**HSG**	Hystero-Salpinogram (graphy)
HIE	Hypoxic Ischaemic Encephalopathy	**HSR**	Homogeneously Staining Region's
HIFX	Hip Fracture	**H'stix**	Haemoglucostix
HIS	Hypertonic Saline Infusion	**HSV**	Herpes Simplex Virus
Hist	Histology / History	**HT**	Haematocrit / Heart / Heart Transplant
HIV	Human Immunodeficiency Virus		/ Height / Hormone Therapy /
HI	Latent Hyperopia		Hypertension / Hypothalamus /
HLR	Hodgkin's Lymphoma		Hyperthyroidism
HLR	Heart Lung Resuscitation	**Ht**	Heart / Height
Hm	Home / Manifest Hyperopia	**5-HT**	5 Hydroxytryptamine (serotonin)
HMSN	Hereditary Motor and Sensory	**HTLV-1**	Human T-Lymphotropic Virus 1
	Neuropathy	**HTLV-2**	Human T-Lymphotropic Virus 2
HN	Head and Neck	**HV**	Hallux Valgus / Has Voided / Heart
HNF	Head, Neck and Face		Volume / Hepatic Vein
hnRNA	Heterogenous Nuclear RNA	**HVS**	High Vaginal Swab
Ho	History of	**HW**	Healing Well / Heart Weight /
HO	History of / House Officer / Hyerbaric		Housewife
	Oxygen	**HX**	History
HOB	Head of Bed	**hx**	history

I	Incisor (tooth)	IAB	Intra-aortic Ballon Counterpulsation
I&A	Irrigation and Aspiration	IABP	Intra-aortic Ballon Pump
I&D	Incision and Drainage	IAC	Internal Auditory Canal
I&E	Internal-External	IAI	Intra-arterial Injection
I&O	Intake and Output (Fluids)	IAM	Internal Auditory Meatus
I&R	Insertion and Removal	ib	in the same place
I/O	In / Out Fluid Balance	IBD	Inflammatory Bowel Disease
IA	Immunoassay / In Addition / Incomplete Abortion / Industrial Accident / Intra-Arterial	IBS	Irritable Bowel Syndrome
		IBW	Ideal Body Weight
		IC	Immunohistochemistry / Informed Consent / Intensive Care / Internal Carotid / Inspiratory Capacity / Irritable Colon
		ICA	Internal Carotid Artery
		ICD	Intra-Uterine Contraceptive Device
		ICH	Intracerebral Haemorrhage
		ICP	Intra-Cranial Pressure
		ICS	Intercostal Space
		ICSH	Interstitial Cell-Stimulating Hormone
		ICU	Intensive Care Unit
		ID	Identification / Identity / Induction Delivery / Infectious Disease / Initial Diagnosis / Intradermal
		ID_{50}	Median Infective Dose
		id	the same
		id.ac	the same as
		IDDM	Insulin Dependent Diabetes Mellitus
		IDL	Intermediate-Density Lipoprotein
		IDM	Infant of Diabetic Mother Indoxuridine
		IE	Inner Ear
		IF	Internal Fixation
		if.nec	if necessary

IQ
Intelligence Quotient

27

IG	Immune Globulin / Insulin and Glucose / Irritable Gut	**IQ**	Intelligence Quotient
IGF	Insulin-like Growth Factors	**IR**	Immune Response
IGT	Impaired Glucose Tolerance	**IRDS**	Idiopathic Respiratory Distress Syndrome
IGTN	Ingrown Toe Nail	**IRV**	Inspiratory Reserve Volume
Ig	Immunoglobulin (IgA, IgD, IgE, IgG, IgM)	**IS**	In Situ / Infant Size / Intercostal Space
IH	Incompletely Healed / Infectious Hepatitis / Internal Haemorrhaging	**is**	in situ / isolated
		isch	ischaemia
IHD	Ischaemic Heart Disease	**ISQ**	In Status Quo
IL	Illness / Inspiratory Load / Interleukin	**ISS**	Injury Severity Scale
IM	Intramuscular	**IT**	Immunotherapy / Insulin Therapy / Intensive Therapy
IMP	Inosine Monophosphate		
ImD$_{50}$	Median Immunizing Dose	**ITV**	Initial Target Volume
Imp	Possible Diagnosis or Impression	**IU**	Intrauterine
IMV	Intermittent Mandatory Ventilation	**IUCD**	Intrauterine Contraceptive Device
Inc	Increased	**IUD**	Intrauterine Death / Intrauterine Device
Inf	Infection	**IUGR**	Intrauterine Growth Restriction
Inj	Injection	**iv**	intravenous
ICU	Intensive Care Unit	**IV**	In Vitro / Intravenous
INR	International Normalised Ratio (clotting ability)	**IVC**	Intravenous Cholangiography
		IVD	Intervertebral Disc
IO	Intestinal Obstruction	**IVDA**	Intravenous Drug Abuse
IOD	Injury on Duty	**IVF**	In Vitro Fertilisation / Intravenous Fluid
IOFB	Intraocular Foreign Body	**IVH**	Intraventricular Haemorrhage
IP	Intraperitoneal / Isoelectric Point	**IVI**	Intravenous Infusion
IPPB	Intermittent Positive Pressure Breathing	**IVP**	Intravenous Pyelogram
IPPV	Intermittent Positive Pressure Ventilation	**IX**	Ion Exchange
		Ix	Investigation
IPV	Poliovirus Vaccine Inactivated	**IXC**	Ion Exchange Chromatography

J/K

J	Joule	**K**	Absolute Zero / Constant / Potassium / Vitamin K / Kelvin
JCV	JC Virus		
JVP	Jugular Venous Pulse	**KB**	Ketone Body / Knee Brace

KF	Kidney Function
Kg	Kilogram
khz	Kilohertz / 1000 Hertz
KJ	Knee Jerk
Kj	Knee Jerk
Km	Michaelis Constant
Kn	Knee
KO	Knocked Out
KOH	Potassium Hydroxide
KOL	Kiss of Life
KT	Kidney Transplant
KUB	Kidneys, Ureters and Bladder
kV	Kilovolt / 1000 Volts
KVO	Keep Vein Open
kVp	Kilovolts Peak

KJ
Knee Jerk

L

L	Lateral / Left / Length / Litre / Lumbar
l	length / litre
L$_1$	First Lumbar Vertebra
L$_2$	Second Lumbar Vertebra, and so on
L Ant	Left Anterior
L Post	Left Posterior
L&D	Labour and Delivery
L&R	Left and Right
L&W	Living and Well
L-dopa	Levodopa
L/R FT	Liver / Renal Function Tests
LA	Left Arm / Left Atrial / Local Anaesthetic
LAM	Laminectomy
LAO	Large Airway Obstruction / Lower Airway Obstruction
LAP	Laparoscopy / Laparotomy / Left Atrial Pressure / Leukocyte Alkaline Phosphatase
LAS	Lower Abdominal Surgery
LASIK	Laser-Assisted in-situ Keratomileusis
LAT	Lateral
LATS	Long-Acting Thyroid Stimulator
LAWK	Last Week
LB	Live Birth / Liver Biopsy / Load Bearing / Lung Biopsy
lb	Pound
LBB	Left Breast Biopsy
LBBB	Left Bundle Branch Block
LBD	Large Bile Duct / Left Brain Damage
LBI	Low Back Injury
LBM	Last Bowel Movement / Loose Bowel Movement
LBP	Low Back Pain

LBW
Low Birth Weight

LF	Left Foot / Low Fat		
LFA	Left Femoral Artery / Left Frontoanterior (foetal position)		
LFD	Low Forceps Delivery		
LFP	Left Frontoposterior (foetal position)		
LFT	Liver Function Test / Left Frontotransverse (foetal position)		
LGA	Large for Gestational Age		
lg	large / leg / long		
LGN	Long Gamma Nail		
LGT	Lowered Glucose Tolerance		
LH	Left Hand / Left Heart / Lower Half / Luteinising Hormone		
LHB	Left Heart Bypass		
LHF	Left Heart Failure		
LHG	Left Hand Grip		
LHR	Laparoscopic Hernia Repair		
LHS	Left Hand Side		
LI	Large Intestine		
LIB	Lower Intestinal Bleeding		
LIC	Left Internal Carotid		
LID	Low Iodine Diet		
LIF	Leukocyte Inhibitory Factor / Left Iliac Fossa		
LK	Left Kidney		
LL	Left Lateral / Left Leg / Left Lower / Left Lung / Lower Limb		
LLA	Lower Limb Amputation		
LLC	Low Leukocyte Count		
LLL	Left Lower Leg / Left Lower Limb / Left Lower Lobe		
LLQ	Left Lower Quadrant		
LLx	Left Lower Extremity		
LMA	Left Mento Antein (position of foetus)		
LMF	Lymphocyte Mitogenic Factor		
LMP	Last Menstrual Period / Left Mento Posterior (position of foetus)		
LMT	Left Mento Transverse (position of foetus)		
LN	Lymph Node		

LBW Low Birth Weight
LC Liver Cirrhosis / Lung Cancer
LCA Left Carotid Artery / Left Coronary Artery
LCAT Lecithin-Cholesterol Acyltransferase
LCC Left Common Carotid
LCD Low Calcium Diet / Low Calorie Diet / Low Cholesterol Diet
LCH Left Cerebral Hemisphere
LCIS Lobular Carcinoma in situ
LCT Liver Cell Tumour
LD Labour and Delivery / Liver Disease
LDH L-lactate Dehydrogenase
LDIH Left Direct Inguinal Hernia
LDL Low Density Lipoprotein (cholesterol)
LD$_{50}$ Median Lethal Dose
LE Lupus Erythematosus / Left Eye
LEA Lumbar Epidural Anaesthesia
LEM Lateral Eye Movement

LWB
Low Weight Bearing

	Lower Respiratory Tract Infection
LS	Left Side / Lumbar Spine
LSA	Left Sacro Anterior (position of foetus) /
LNB	Large Needle Biopsy / Liver Needle
	Biopsy
LNE	Lymph Node Enlargement
LNPF	Lymph Node Permeability Factor
LNS	Large Volume Normal Saline
lo.cal	low calorie
LOA	Left Occipito Anterior (position of
	foetus)
LOB	Loss of Balance
LOC	Loss of Consciousness
LOM	Left Otitis Media / Limitation of Motion
LOP	Left Occipito Posterior (position of
	foetus)
LOS	Length of Stay
LOT	Left Occipito Transverse (position of
	foetus)
LOV	Loss of Vision
LOW	Loss of Weight
LP	Lateral Posterior / Liver Plasma /
	Lumbar Puncture
LPA	Left Pulmonary Artery
LPM	Litres per Minute
LPS	Last Pap Smear
LPV	Lymphotropic Papovavirus
LRA	Left Renal Artery
LRD	Lower Respiratory Tract Disease
LRT	Liver Transplant / Lower Respiratory
	Tract

	Left Subclavian Artery
LSC	Lower Segment Caesarian
LScA	Left Scapulo Anterior (position of foetus)
LScP	Left Scapulo Posterior (position of foetus)
LSCS	Lower Segment Caesarian Section
LSD	Low Sodium Diet / Lysergic Acid
	Diethylamide
LSK	Liver, Spleen and Kidneys
LSP	Left Sacro Posterior (position of foetus)
LST	Left Sacro Transverse (position of foetus)
LT	Lumbar Traction
LTF	Lymphocyte Transforming Factor
LTI	Laryngoscopy and Tracheal Intubation
LTL	Left Temporal Lobe
LU	Left Upper
LUA	Left Upper Arm
LUL	Left Upper Limb / Left Upper Lobe
LUQ	Left Upper Quadrant
LUT	Lower Urinary Tract
LV	Left Venticle / Lumbar Vertebra
LVAD	Left Ventricular Assist Device
LVB	Left Ventricular Bypass
LVF	Left Ventricular Failure
LVH	Left Ventricular Hypertrophy
LVO	Left Ventricular Obstruction
LW	Low
LWB	Low Weight Bearing
LX	Lower Extremity

M

M	Male / Married / Minute / Month / Mother	**ME**	Middle Ear
M Pads	Maternity Pads	**M-E**	Monitoring and Evaluation
M&F	Male and Female / Mother and Father	**MED**	Minimum Effective Dose
M&R	Measure and Record	**MEN**	Multiple Endocrine Neoplasia
MA	Megaloblastic Anaemia / Mental Age	**mEq**	milliequivalent
MAC	Membrane Attack Complex	**MET**	Methionine
Mane	In The Morning	**MeV**	Megaelectron Volt / One Million (10 6) Electron Volts
MAO	Monoamine Oxidase	**MG**	Myesthenia Gravis
MAOI	Monoamine Oxidase Inhibitor	**Mg**	Magnesium / Milligram
MAP	Mean Airway Pressure / Mean Aortic Pressure / Mean Arterial Pressure	**MH**	Medical History
		MHC	Major Histocompatibility Complex
MAT	Multifocal Atrial Tachycardia	**MHZ**	Megahertz / One Million (10 6) Hertz
mb	mix well	**MI**	Mental Illness / Mitral Incompetence / Myocardial Infarction / Myocardial Ischaemia
MBA	Mother Baby Assessment		
MBP	Mean Blood Pressure		
mC	millicurie	**MIRL**	Membrane Inhibitor of Reactive Lysis
MC&S	Microbiology, Culture and Sensitivity	**ML**	Midline
MCA	Main Coronary Artery / Middle Carotid Artery	**MLD**	Minimum Lethal Dose / Median Lethal Dose
MCH	Mean Cell Haemoglobin / Mean Corpuscular Haemoglobin	**MI**	Millilitre
		MM	Multiple Myeloma
MCHC	Mean Cell Haemoglobin Concentration / Mean Corpuscular Haemoglobin Concentration	**MMIHS**	Megacystis-Microcolon-Intestinal Hypoperistalsis Syndrome
		mm	millimetre
MCLE	Multicystic Leukoencephalomalacia	**MMR**	Measles-Mumps-Rubella (vaccine)
MCP	Membrane Cofactor Protein	**Mn**	Manganese / Midnight
MCV	Mean Cell Volume / Mean Corpuscular Volume	**MND**	Motor Neuron Disease
		MO	Medical Officer / Month
MDA	Methylenedioxyamphetamine	**mo**	month
MDF	Myocardial Depressant Factor	**MOF**	Multiple Myeloma
MDMA	3,4-Methylendeioxymethamphetamine	**M of I**	Mechanism of Injury
MDR	Minimum Daily Requirement	**MON**	Middle of the Night / Monitoring

MONO	Monocytes	**MSH**	Melanocyte-Stimulating Hormone /
mOsm	milliosmole weight		Melanophore-Stimulating Hormone
6-MP	Mercaptopurine	**MSL**	Meconium Stained Liquor
MPD	Maximum Permissible Dose	**MSOF**	Multiple System Organ Failure
MPO	Myeloperoxide	**MSU**	Mid Stream Urine Specimen
MPS	Mononuclear Phagocyte System	**MSUD**	Maple Syrup Urine Disease
MPV	Mean Platelet Volume	**MTB**	Mycobacterium Tuberculosis
MR	May Repeat / Mental Retardation /	**mtDNA**	Mitochondrial DNA
	Mitral Regurgitation	**MUA**	Manipulation Under Anaesthesia
mR	milliroentgen	**MV**	Mechanical Ventilation / Minute Volume
MRA	Magnetic Resonance Angiography	**mV**	millivolt
MRB	Manual Resuscitation Bag	**μV**	microvolt
MRI	Magnetic Resonance Imaging	**MVB**	Manual Ventilation Bag
mRNA	Messenger RNA	**MVI**	Motor Vehicle Injury
MROP	Manual Removal of Placenta	**MVP**	Mitral Valve Prolapse
MRSA	Methicillin Resistant Staphylococcus	**MVR**	Mitral Valve Replacement
	Aureus	**MVS**	Mitral Valve Stenosis
MS	Mass Spectometry / Mitral Stenosis /	**MW/**	Molecular Weight
	Multiple Sclerosis / Mitra Stenosis	**Mol WT**	
Ms	Murmurs	**Mx**	Medical History / Medication

MSU
Mid Stream Urine Specimen

33

N

N	Newton / Nitrogen / Normal / Number
NA	Avogadro's Number
Na	Sodium
NAA	No Apparent Abnormalities
NAB	Needle Aspiration Biopsy
NAD	Nicotinamide Adenine Dinucleotide / No Abnormality Detected
NADP	Pihydropyrimidine Dehydrogenase
NAF	No Abnormal Findings
nag	nanogram
NAI	No Action Indicated / Non Accidental Injury
NAK	Nothing Abnormal Known
NAPB	Negative Airway Pressure Breathing
NAR	No Action Required
NAT	No Action Taken
NB	Needle Biopsy
NBD	No Brain Damage
NBF	New Bone Formation
NBI	No Bony Injury
NBM	Advised To Eat Nothing / Nil By Mouth / No Bowel Movement
NBS	Normal Blood Serum / Normal Bowel Sounds
NBTE	Nonbacterial Thrombotic Endocarditis
NC	Nasal Cannula
NCB	Needle Core Biopsy
NCS	Nerve Conduction Study
Nd:YAG	Neodymium : Yurium-Aluminium -Garnet
NDA	No Data Available

NDD	Non Insulin Dependent
NDF	No Diagnostic Findings
nDNA	Nuclear DNA
NDR	Non Drug Resistant
NED	No Evidence of Disease
NEFA	Non Esterified Fatty Acids
NEG	Negative
NEM	No Evidence of Malignancy
NEU	Neutrophils
NFD	Non Fat Diet
NFG	Normal Fasting Glucose
NFH	Negative Family History
NFT	No Further Treatment
NG	Nasogastric

NAD
No Abnormality Detected

ng	nanogram		Analgesic (or agent)
NGT	Nasogastric Tube / Normal Glucose	**NSAID**	Non Steroid Anti-Inflammatory Drug
	Tolerance	**NSC**	No Significant Change
NH₃	Ammonia	**NSCLC**	Non-Small Cell Lung Carcinoma / Cancer
NHD	No Heart Disease		No Sign Detected
NHI	No Head Injuries	**NSD**	Normal Spontaneous Delivery
NHO	No History of	**nsec**	nanosecond
NIA	No Information Available	**NSS**	Normal Saline Solution
NIBP	Non Invasive Blood Pressure	**NTD**	Noted
NIC	Neonatal Intensive Care	**NTI**	Nasotracheal Intubation
NIDDM	Non Insulin Dependent Diabetes	**NVD**	Normal Vaginal Delivery
	Mellitus	**NVS**	No Visual Symptoms
Nil Else	Nothing Else Worth Recording		
NKA	No Known Allergy		
NLB	Needle Liver Biopsy		
NLS	No Lesion Seen		
nm	nanometer		
NMB	Needle Muscle Biopsy / Neuromuscular		
	Block		
NMC	Normal Menstrual Cycle		
NMI	Normal Male Infant		
NMP	Normal Menstrual Period		
nn	nerves		
NNJ	Neonatal Jaundice		
NNO	Neonatal Death		
NOAD	No Other Abnormality Detected		
Nocte	At Night		
NOF	Neck of Femur		
NOK	Next of Kin		
NPN	Non Protein Nitrogen		
NPO	Nil By Mouth		
NPR	Normal Pulse Rate		
NPU	Not Passed Urine		
NREM	Non Rapid Eye Movement		
NRM	Normal Range of Motion		
NS	Normal Saline		
N/S	No show / Normal Saline		
NSA	No Salt Added / No Significant		
	Abnormality		
NSAIA	Non Steroidal Anti Inflammatory		

NIDDM
Non Insulin Dependent Diabetes Mellitus

O

O	Without	**ORN**	Orthopaedic Nurse
O/E	On Examination	**OS**	Left eye / mouth / bone
o/n	overnight	**OT**	Osteoarthritis / Outpatient Appointment
O₂	Oxygen		/ Ocular Albinism
OA	Osteoarthritis / Outpatient Appointment	**OTC**	Over The Counter
	/ Ocular Albinism	**OU**	Each Eye
OAD	Obstructive Airway Disease / Once a Day	**OZ**	Ounce
OAF	Osteoclast Activating Factor		
OAO	On and Off		
OBA	Oxygen Breathing Apparatus		
OB/Obs	Obstetrics		
OBT	Oral Body Temperature		
OCA	Oculocutaneous Albinism		
OCB/D	Obsessive Compulsive Behaviour / Disease / Disorder		
Occ	Occasional		
OD	Once a Day / Right Eye / Overdose		
ODOD	Oculodentodigital Dysplasia		
OE	Once in the Evening		
OETT	Oral Endotracheal Tube		
OHR	Open Hernia Repair		
OHS	Open Heart Surgery		
OI	Osteogenesis Imperfecta		
oint	ointment		
OL	Left Eye		
OLD	Obstructive Lung Disease		
OM	Once in the Morning / Otitis Media		
OPC	Outpatient Clinic		
OPD	Outpatient Department		
OPV	Opliovirus Vaccine Live Oral		
OR	Open Reduction / Operating Room		
ORIF	Open Reduction and Internal Fixation		

ORN
Orthopaedic Nurse

P

P	Prosthetics / Pulse / Phosphorus / Posterior / Premolar / Pupil / Power / Pressure
p	After Meals
P₁	Parental Generation
P₂	Pulmonic Second Sound
P&O	Prosthetics and Orthopaedics
P&P	Pin and Plate
P/E	Physical Examination
P/E	Patient Examination
PA	Posteroranterior / Pulmonary Artery / Physician Assistant
PABA	P-Aminobenzoic Acid
PAE	Pulmonary Air Embolism
Paed	Paediatrician
PAF	Platelet Activating Factor
PAHA	P-Aminohippuric Acid

PAEDIATRIC SURGICAL UNIT

PaO₂	Partial Pressure of Oxygen
pap	Papanicolaou Smear
PAI	Plasminogen Activator Inhibitor
PASA	P-Aminosalicylic Acid
PAWP	Peak Airway Pressure / Pulmonary Artery Wedge Pressure
PBI	Protein-Bound Iodine
PC	Phosphocreatine
pc	after meals
PCA	Prostrate Cancer
PCB	Polychlorinated Biphenyl
PCE	Pseudocholinesterase
PCL	Posterior Cruciate Ligament
PCOS	Polycystic Ovary Syndrome
PCO₂	Partial Pressure of Carbon Dioxide
PCP	Phencyclidine
PCR	Polymerase Chain Reaction
PCS	Post Concussion Syndrome
PCT	Porphyria Cutanea Tarda
PCV	Packed-Cell Volume

PSU
Paediatric Surgical Unit

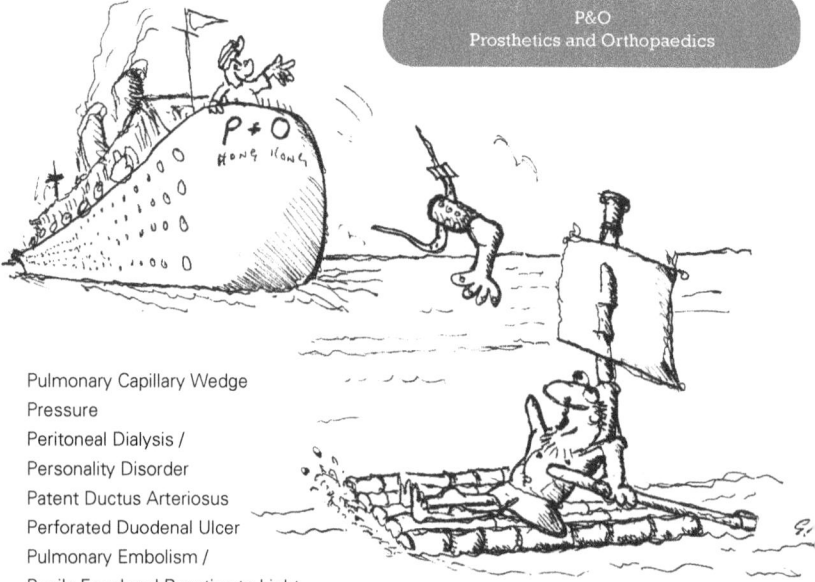

P&O
Prosthetics and Orthopaedics

PCWP	Pulmonary Capillary Wedge Pressure
PD	Peritoneal Dialysis / Personality Disorder
PDA	Patent Ductus Arteriosus
PDU	Perforated Duodenal Ulcer
PEARL	Pulmonary Embolism / Pupils Equal and Reactive to Light
PEEP	Positive End-Expiratory Pressure
PEF	Peak Expiratory Flow
PEG	Penumoencephalography / Polyethyleneglycol
PET	Positive Emission Tomography
PFH	Positive Family History
PFT	Pulmonary Function Tests
PGL	Plasma Glucose Level
PGU	Peptic Gastric Ulcer / Perforated Gastric Ulcer
pH	Acidity / Alkalinity / Hydrogen Ion Concentration
PHD	Pulmonary Heart Disease
PHI	Past History of Illness
PHT	Patient History / Pulmonary Hypertension
PHx	Patient History
PI	Pulmonary Incompetence

PICU	Paediatric Intensive Care Unit
PID	Pelvic Inflammatory Disease / Prolapse Intervertebral Disc
PIE	Apyrexial
PKU	Phenylketonuria
plc	platelet count
PLR	Positive Leg Raising
PLT	Platelets
PM	After Death / Post Mortem
PMHx	Past Medical History
PMI	Point of Maximal Impulse (of the heart)
PMMA	Polymethyl Methacrylate
PMS	Post Menstrual Stress
PNB	Percutaneous Needle Biopsy
PND	Persistent Nasal Discharge / Post Natal Depression
PNET	Primitive Neuroectodermal Tumour
PNS	Parasympathetic Nervous System

PO	Oral / Orally, By Mouth	**PTB**	Pulmonary Tuberculosis
POB	Place of Birth / Post-Operative Bleeding	**PTC**	Percutaneous Transhepatic
POD	Post-Operative Day / Pouch of Douglas		Cholangiography / Plasma
POI	Post-Operative Infection		Thromboplastin Complex
POL	Premature Onset of Labour	**PTH**	Parathyroid Hormone
POP	Plaster of Paris	**PTSD**	Post Traumatic Stress Disorder / Post
POR	Problem-Oriented Record		Traumatic Stress Disease
POT	Post-Operative Treatment	**PTT**	Partial Thromboblastin Time
PPA	Palpation, Percussion, Auscultation	**PU**	Passed Urine / Peptic Ulcer
PPD	Packs per Day / Permanent Partial	**PUBS**	Percutaneous Umbilical Blood Sampling
	Disability / Postpartum Depression /	**PUFA**	Polyunsaturated Fatty Acid
	Purified Protein Derivative	**PV**	Per Vaginum
PPH	Post Partum Haemorrhage	**PVC**	Polyvinyl Chloride
ppm	parts per million	**PVD**	Peripheral Vascular Disease
PPU	Perforated Peptic Ulcer	**PVP**	Polyvinylpyrroliodine
PR	Per Rectum / Prosthion / Pulmonic	**PVP-I**	Povidone-Iodine
	Regurgitation	**PVS**	Permanent Vegetative State
Pr	Praseodymium / Presbyopia / Prism	**Px**	Prognosis
PRA	Panel-Reactive Antibody	**PxR**	Pelvic X-Ray
Pre Med	Pre Surgery		
Prl / PRL	Prolactin		
PR(O)M	Premature Rupture of Membranes		
Pro-uk	Prourokinase		
PRN	as needed / According to		
	Circumstances		
prn	as needed		
PS	Partial Saturation / Pulmonary Stenosis		
PSA	Prostate-Specific Antigen		
PSF	Posterior Spinal Fusion		
PSP	Peak Systolic Pressure		
PSU	Paediatric Surgical Unit		
PSVT	Paroxysmal Supraventricular		
	Tachycardia		
PT/pt	Physiotherapy / Premature		
	Termination of Pregnancy /		
	Prothrombin Time /		
	Patient		
PTA	Post Traumatic Amnesia / Prior to		
	Admission / Plasma Thromboplastin		
	Component		

PCS
Post Concussion Syndrome

Q

q	symbol for long arm of chromosome / every day	q.s	sufficient quantity
Q_{10}/Q	Ubiquinone	qh	every hour
QDS	Receiving Medication Four Times per day	qhs	every bedtime
		qid	four times a day
q.h.s	every night at bedtime	qod	every other day
		qv	as much as you wish

R

R	Rate / Respiration / Electrical Resistance .
r	rhythm / right / roentgen / ring chromosome
R/O	Rule Out
R/T	Ryles Tube
R/t	Prescription with Treatment
RA	Rheumatoid Arthritis
RA/RAW	Airway Resistance
RAB	Right Atrial Bypass
RAI	Radioactive Iodine Therapy
RAS	Renal Artery Stenosis
RAST	Radioallergosorbent Test
RAT	Right Atrial Tachycardia
RAV	Rous-Associated Virus
RBBB	Right Bundle Branch Block
RBC	Red Blood Cell / Red Blood Corpuscle
RC	Retrograde Cholangiography
RCC	Red Cell Count / Renal Cell Carcinoma

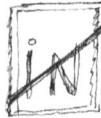

R/O
Rule Out

RCG	Radio Cardiography
RCS	Repeat Caesarian Section
RCT	Radiotherapy and Chemotherapy
RD	Retinal Detachment
RDA	Recommended Daily Allowance
RDD	Recommended Daily Dose
RDS	Respiratory Distress Syndrome
RDT	Renal Dialysis Therapy
RDW	Red Cell Distribution Width
REM	Rapid Eye Movement
ren	kidney
rel	relative
RES	Reticuloendothelial System
Resp	Respiratory Rate
RF	Rheumatoid Factor
RFA	Reason for Admission / Right Femoral Artery / Front to Anterior (position)
RFI	Request for Information
RFL	Right Frontal Lobe
RFM	Retention of Foetal Membranes
RFP	Right Front to Posterior (position)
RFT	Renal Function Tests / Right Front to Transverse (position)
Rh	Rhesus Factor
RHB	Right Heart Bypass
RHD	Rheumatic Heart Disease
RHF	Right Heart Failure
RHR	Resting Heart Rate
RIND	Reversible Ischaemic Neurological Deficit
RIST	Radioimmunosorbent Test
RIT	Radioimmunotherapy
RLE	Right Lower Extremity
RLF	Retrolental Fibroplasia / Retrolental Factor
RLL	Right Lower Limb / Right Lower Lobe
RLQ	Right Lower Quadrant
RMA	Right Mento Anterior (position)

RUE
Right Upper Extremity

RML	Right Middle Lobe
RMP	Right Mento Posterior (position)
RMT	Right Mento Transverse (position)
RNA	Ribo Nucleic Acid
RNase	RIbonuclease
ROA	Right Occipito Anterior (position)
ROM	Right Otitis Media / Rupture of Membranes
ROP	Right Occipito Posterior (position)
RPF	Renal Plasma Flow
RQ	Respiratory Quotient
RR	Respiratory Rate
rRNA	Ribosomal RNA
RSA	Right Sacro Anterior (position)
RSB	Rapid and Shallow Breathing
RScA	Right Scapulo Anterior (position)
RScP	Right Scapulo Posterior (position)
RSDS	Reflex Sympathetic Dystrophy

41

	Syndrome	**RU-486**	Mifepristone
RSP	Right Sacro Posterior (position)	**RUE**	Right Upper Extremity
RST	Right Sacro Transverse (position)	**RUL**	Right Upper Limb
RSV	Rous Sarcoma Virus / Respiratory	**RUQ**	Right Upper Quadrant
	Syncitial Virus	**RV**	Residual Volume
RT	Radiotherapy	**RVA**	Rabies Vaccine Absorbed
RTA	Renal Tubular Acidosis / Road Traffic	**RVAD**	Right Ventricular Assist Device
	Accident	**RVF**	Right Ventricular Failure
RTF	Resistance Transfer Factor	**RVH**	Right Ventricular Hypertrophy
RTI	Respiratory Tract Infection	**RVT**	Renal Vein Thrombosis

S

S	Sacrum / Sulfur / Sacral Vertebrae (S1-S5) / Siemens / Spherical Lens	**SCU-PA**	Single Chain Urokinase-type Plasminogen Activator
s	without	**SD**	Skin Dose
S$_1$	First Sacral Vertebra	**SDH**	Subdural Haematoma
S$_2$	Second Sacral Vertebra, etc	**SDS**	Sudden Death Syndrome / Sodium
SA	Sinoatrial		Dodecyl Sulfate
S/B	Seen By	**SE**	Standard Error
SAD	Seasonal Affective Disease	**SED**	Skin Erythema Dose
SAH	Subarachnoid Haemorrhage	**SGA**	Small for Gestational Age
SaO$_2$	Oxygen Saturation	**SGOT**	Serum Glutamic Oxaloacetic
SAP	Serum Alkaline Phosphatase		Transaminase
SAS	Signs and Symptoms	**SGPT**	Serum Glutamate Pyruvate
SBE	Shortness of Breath on Exertion /		Transaminase
	Subacute Bacterial Endocarditis	**SHL**	Sensorineural Hearing Loss
SBP	Systolic Blood Pressure	**SHx**	Social History
SC	Sub-Cutaneous	**SIB**	Stillbirth
SCA	Sickle Cell Anaemia	**SIADH**	Syndrome of Inappropriate Antidiuretic
SCC	Spinal Cord Compression / Squamous		Hormone
	Cell Carcinoma	**SID**	Sudden Inexplicable Death
SCID	Severe Combined Immunodeficiency	**sid**	once a day
	Disease	**SIDS**	Suddent Infant Death Syndrome
SCLC	Small Cell Lung Cancer	**SII**	Self Inflicted Injury

SIMV	Synchronous Intermittent Mandatory Ventilation
SISI	Short Increment Sensitivity Index
SIV	Simian Immunodeficiency Virus
SKSD	Streptokinase Streptodornase
SL	Sub-Lingual
SLB	Short Leg Brace
SLE	Systemic Lupus Erythematosus
SLR	Straight Leg Raising
SLV	Since Last Visit
SMA	Spinal Muscular Atrophy / Superior Mesenteric Arteriography
SMR	Severe Mental Retardation
SMV	Superior Mesenteric Venography
SNH	Sensorineural Hearing Loss
SNS	Sympathetic Nervous System
SOB	Shortness of Breath
SOBOE	Shortness of Breath on Exertion
SOL	Spontaneous Onset of Labour
Sol	Solution
SOS	Can be repeated once if urgent / if necessary
SPCA	Serum Prothrombin Conversion Acceleration
SPECT	Single-Photon Emission Computed Tomography
SPM	Sputum
SpT	Spinal Tap
SR	Sinus Rhythm
SRH	Somatotropin-Releasing Hormone
SRIF/SS	Somatostatin
SRM	Spontaneous Rupture of Membranes
SROM	Spontaneous Rupture of Membranes
SRR	Surgical Recovery Room
SRS-A	Slow-Reacting Substance of Anaphylaxis
SS	One Half

SSEP	Somatosensory Evoked Potential
SSI	Surgical Site Infection
SSRI	Selective Serotonin Reuptake Inhibitor
ST	Sinus Tachycardia
St	Stoke
STAT	Immediately
STB	Stable
STD	Sexually Transmitted Disease / Short Term Disability / Standard
STM	Streptomycin
STI	Systolic Time Interval
STOP	Miscarriage (Spontaneous Termination of Pregnancy)
SubT#T	Sub-Trochanteric Fracture of Femur
sum	let it be taken
SVCO	Superior Vena Cava Obstruction
SVT	Superficial Vein Thrombosis / Supraventricular Tachycardia
SWD	Short Wave Diathermy

SOS
Can be repeated once if urgent

T

T	Temperature / Tesla / Thymine or Thymidine
t	time
T_1	First Thoracic Vertebra
T_2	Second Thoracid Vertebra
$T_{1/2}$	Half-life
$t_{1/2}$	half-life
T3	Thyroxene
T/#	Trochanteric Fracture
TA	Therapeutic Abortion / Traffic Accident / Tricuspid Atresia / Toxin-Antitoxin
TAA	Thoracic Aortic Aneurism / Total Amino Acids Thin Needle Aspiration Biopsy
TAH	Total Abdominal Hysterectomy
TAO	Total Acid Output
TAP	Total Alkaline Phosphatase
TAV	Tricuspid Aortic Valve
TB	Tuberculosis
TBA	To be added
TBC	To be continued / Total Bacterial Count / Total Blood Cholesterol
TBG	Thyroxine Binding Globulin
TBL	Total Blood Loss
TBI	Traumatic Brain Injuries
TBS	Total Body Scan
TBV	Total Blood Volume
TDS	Receiving Medication Three times a Day
TD_{50}	Median Toxic Dose
TEC	Total Erythrocyte Count
Teds	Stockings That Prevent Blood Clots
TEE	Transoesophageal Echocardiography

TF	Tube Feeding
TFCC	Triangular Fibrocartilage Complex
TFI	Total Food Intake
TFT	Thyroid Function Tests

THR
Total Hip Replacement

TFU	To Follow Up		**TOT**	Total Operating Time
TG	Thyroglobulin		**TP**	Total Protein
TGF	Transforming Growth Factor		**TPN**	Total Parenteral Nutrition
THR	Total Hip Replacement		**TPR**	Temperature, Pulse, Respiration
TIA	Transient Ischaemic Attack		**TPV**	Total Plasma Volume
TIBC	Total Iron Binding Capacity		**TRH**	Thyroid Releasing Hormone /
TID	Times Daily			Thyrotropin-Releasing Hormone /
tid	three times a day			Tricuspid Regurgitation
TKR	Total Knee Replacement		**tRNA**	Transfer RNA
TLC	Total Lymphocyte Count / Total Lung		**TRO**	To Rule Out
	Capacity / Thin-layer Chromatography		**TSA**	Tumour-Specific Antigen
TNB	Thin Needle Biopsy		**TSB**	Total Serum Bilirubin
TND	Term Normal Delivery		**TSD**	Tay-Sachs Disease
TOA	Time of Arrival		**TSH**	Thyroid Stimulating Hormone
TOD	Take off Dose / Time of Day / Time of		**TTD**	Temporary Total Disability
	Death		**TTM**	Total Tumour Mass
TOF	Tetralogy of Fallot		**TTO**	Discharge Medication
TOL	Trial of Labour		**TURP**	Transurethral Reaction of the Prostate
TOM	Tomography		**TWC**	Total White Cell Count
TOP	Termination of Pregnancy		**TWI**	Total Water Intake
TOS	Trial of Scar		**Tx**	Transfer / Treatment

U

U	Uranium, Uracil, Uridine			Tomography
U&Es	Urea and Electrolytes		**UDP**	Uridine Diphosphate
u/o	urinary output		**UK**	Urokinase
U/S	Ultrasound		**UL**	Upper Limb
UA	Urine Analysis		**UMP**	Uridine Monophosphate
UAD	Urinary Acid Output		**UO**	Under Observation
UAL	Urine Alcohol Level		**URD**	Upper Respiratory Disease
UBC	Urinary Bladder Cancer		**URI**	Upper Respiratory Infection
UCC	Uterine Cervical Cancer		**URT**	Upper Respiratory Tract
UCG	Ultracardiography		**URTI**	Upper Respiratory Tract Infection
UCT	Ultrasound Computed		**USD**	Unexplained Sudden Death

USE	Ultrasound Examination	**ut dict**	as directed
USG	Ultrasonography	**UTD**	Up-to-date
US	Ultrasound	**UTP**	Uridine Triphosphate
USI	Upper Small Intestine	**UTI**	Urinary Tract Infection
USS	Ultra Sound Scan	**UV**	Ultraviolet

V

V	Visit At Home Required / Vision / Volt / Volume
v	vein
VAD	Ventricular Assist Device
V/B	Visited By
VAM	Viral Acute Meningitis
VBD	Vaginal Breach Delivery
VBG	Vascular Bone Graft
VBM	Voluntary Bowel Movement
VC	Vital Capacity
VCG	Vectorcardiogram
VD	Venereal Disease
VDH	Valvular Disease of the Heart
VDRL	Screening for Syphylis
VE	Vaginal Examination
VEP	Visual Evoked Potential
VF	Vocal Fremitus
vf	visual field
VFI	Ventricular Flutter
Vfib	Ventricular Fibrillation
VFA	Ventricular Fibrillation Arrest / Visual Functional Assessment
VFL	Ventricular Fibrillation
VHA	Viral Hepatitis A
VHB	Viral Hepatitis B
VHC	Vital Hepatitis C

VHDL	Very-High-Density Lipoprotein
Vit	Vitamin
Vit K	Vitamin K

VR
Vocal Resonance

VLBW	Very Low Birth Weight		**VSA**	Vital Signs Absent
VLDL	Very-Low-Density Lipoprotein		**VSD**	Ventricular Septal Defect
VMA	Vanilylmandelic Acid		**VSS**	Vital Signs Stable
VPB	Ventricular Premature Beat		**VT**	Ventricular Tachycardia
VPC	Ventricular Premature Complex		**v/v**	volume (of solute) per volume (of
VR	Vocal Resonance			solvent)
VRI	Virus Respiratory Infection		**vWF**	von Willebrand's Factor
VS	Vital Signs / Volumetric Solution			

W/X/Z

w	with		**WDWN**	Well Developed Well Nourished
W/wt	Weight		**WLE**	Working Life Expectancy
WBA	Whole Blood Assay		**WR**	Ward Round
WBC	White Blood Cell / Weight Bearing		**w/v**	weight (of solute) per volume (of solvent)
	with Crutches / Whole Blood Count		**XR**	X-Ray
WBD	Will Be Discharged		**X**	Xanthine or Xanthosine
WBH	Whole Blood Haematocrit		**x**	for / unknown
WBI	Whole Body Irradiation		**Xe**	Xenon
WBS	Whole Body Scan		**Zn**	Zinc
WCC	White Cell Count		**Zr**	Zirconium

Signs and Symbols

<	Less than	V	Trigeminal Nerve
>	Greater than	VI	Abducens Nerve
±	More or less / indefinite	VII	Facial Nerve
Δ	Diagnosis, Change	VIII	Vestibulocochlear Nerve
Ψ	Psychiatric	IX	Glossopharyngeal Nerve
↑	Increased / Elevated / Extensor	X	Vagus Nerve
↓	Decreased /Flexor	XI	Accessory Nerve
↑↓	Equivocal	XII	Hypoglossal Nerve
♀	Female	#	Fracture
♂	Male	/40	Pregnancy
−	Absent /Negative	2+	Two weeks overdue
+	Present but depressed / Positive	- 1	1 cm above ischial spine
+ +	Normal	ā	Before
+ + +	Elevated /Increased	c̄	With
?	Possible	p̄	After
©	About	s̄	Without
±	More or Less	Ⓑ	Bilateral
α	Alpha	Ø	None
3/7	Three days	—	Lying
3/12	Three months	⌐	Sitting
I	Olfactory Nerve			Standing
II	Optic Nerve	1°	Primary
III	Occulomotor Nerve	2°	Secondary
IV	Trochlear Nerve	3°	Tertiary

Prefixes

	meaning	examples
a-, an	not, without	*Aplasia, Anoxia*
ab-	away from	*Abduction*
ad-	to, toward	*Adduction*
ambi-	both	*Ambilateral*
ana-	up, towards, apart	*Anatropia*
ante-	before	*Antepartum*
anti-	against, opposing	*Anticoagulant*
brady-	slow	*Bradycardia*
circum-	around	*Circumcision*
contra-	against, opposed	*Contraindicated*
de-	from, down	*Defaecation*
dia-	between, through	*Diaphysis*
dis-	apart, free from	*Dislocated*
ec-, ef-, ex-	out of, from, away from	*Ectopic, Efferent, Excision*
em-, en-	in, into, within	*Embolism, Endoscopy*
end-, endo-, ent-, ento-	within, inside	*Endaural, Endometrium, Enteric, Entorational*
epi-	on, over, upon	*Epidermis*
gyn-	female, woman	*Gynaecological*
hemi-	partial, half	*Hemiparesis*
hetero-	other, different	*Heteroblastic*
hyper-	above, beyond, excessive	*Hyperventilation*
hyp-, hypo-	under, beneath, deficient	*Hypaxial, Hypodermic*
im-. in-	in, into, within, not	*Implant, Infusion*
infra-	below, beneath	*Infraorbital*
inter-	between	*Intercostal*
intra-	within, into	*Intraocular*
mal-	bad, abnormal	*Malabsorption*
mega-, megalo-	big, large	*Megaloblast*
mes-, meso-	middle	*Mesencephalotomy, Mesomorph*
meta-	change	*Metastasis*
micro-	small	*Microorganism*
multi-	many	*Multicystic*
neo-	new, recent	*Neonatal, neoplasm*

oligo-	little, few	*Oliguria*
pan-	all	*Pancarditis*
para-	beside, beyond, after	*Parathyroidal*
per-	through, excessive	*Percutaneous*
peri-	around. surrounding	*Peripartum*
poly-	many, much, excessive	*Polycystic*
post-	after, behind	*Postpartum*
pre-, pro-	before, in front of	*Precursor, Prognosis*
pseud-, pseudo-	false	*Pseudoepilepsy*
pyo-	pus	*Pyogenic*
re-, retro-	backward, behind, again	*Recuperation, Retrograde*
semi-	half	*Semipermeable*
steno-	narrow	*Stenosis*
sub-	under, below, beneath	*Subclavian*
super-, supra-	above	*Superficial, Supraorbital*
tachy-	fast	*Tachycardia*

Suffixes

	meaning	examples
-ac, -al, -ic, -ar, -ial, -ary	related to, located in	*iliac, vagal, thrombic, auricular, arterial, biliary*
-ous, -tic, -eal	pertaining to	*venous, optic, corneal*
-algia	pain	*neuralgia*
-ase	enzyme	*diastase*
-asthemia	weakness	*myasthemia*
-clasia, -clast	break	*osteoclasia (clast)*
-cle, -cule, -ole	small	*vescicle, molecule, arteriole*
-coccus	berry shaped	*streptococcus*
-crine	separate, secrete	*endocrine*
-crit	to separate	*haematocrit*
-cyte	cell	*lymphocyte, erythrocyte*
-ectomy	surgical removal	*appendectomy*
-emia	blood condition	*hyponatremia*
-esis, -ia	disease	*metastesis, presbyopia*
-gen	producing, causing	*pyrogen*
-gram	record	*cystogram*

-graph	instruments that record	*cardiotocograph*
-iac	person afflicted with	*hypochondriac*
-ible, -ile	capable, able	*reversible, immobile*
-ician	one who	*physician*
-ism, -osis, -tion, -sis, -iasis, -sia	state or condition	*hyperthyroidism, thrombosis, herniation, sepsis psoriasis, eplesia*
-ist, -ologist	a specialist in	*optometrist, cardiologist*
-ium	membrane	*epithelium, endometrium*
-lysis, -lytic	destroy	*haemodialysis, haemolytic*
-ma	disease	*carcinoma medulloblastoma*
-malacia	softening	*encephalomalacia*
-megaly	enlargement	*splenomegaly*
-metry	measurement	*optometry*
-morph	form, shape	*endomorph*
-oma	tumour	*llymphoma*
-opsy	to view	*biopsy*
-oxia	oxygen	*hypoxia*
-paresis	slight paralysis	*hemiparesis*
-pathy	disease	*adenopathy, cardiomyopathy*
-pepsia	digestion	*dyspepsia*
-phoria	feeling	*euphoria*
-plasm	formation, development	*neoplasm*
-plasty	surgical repair	*enteroplasty*
-plegia	paralysis	*quadriplegia*
-pnoea	breathing	*apnoea*
-porosis	passage	*osteoporosis*
-ptosis	drooping	*proptosis*
-rrhage	excessive flow	*haemorrhage*
-rrhoea	flow, discharge	*diarrhoea*
-sarcoma	malignant tumour	*lymphosarcoma*
-sclerosis	hardening	*arteriosclerosis*
-scope	instrument for examining	*laryngoscope*
-scopy	visual examination	*laryngoscopy*
-stomy	surgical opening	*tracheostomy*
-tes, -itis	inflammation	*ascites, poliomyelitis*
-tomy	cutting, incision	*tracheaostomy*
-trophy	nourishment, development	*hypertrophy*
-ule	little	*molecule*

Ranges of Motion

Orthopaedic reports often contain information as to the range of motion of an affected part of the patient's body without any reference to normal values, thus making it impossible, in the absence of live evidence from an expert, to determine the degree of disability. This section is intended as a guide to normal values, subject to the qualification that there is no internationally adopted standard since the ranges are dependent upon various factors such as age, ethnicity, the conditions under which studies were performed etc.

For this reason, normal ranges of motion from five different sources are set out. It should be noted that some sources provide for a range beginning with a zero value, whilst others do not. For example, one source for extension of the neck may provide for a figure of 55 degrees, whilst another may provide 0 - 55 degrees. Further, figures often appear to differ greatly depending on whether or not measurements were taken from neutral positions.

NECK	1	2	3	4	5
Flexion (touch sternum with chin)	—	—	—	—	60/ - / - /40
Extension (point up with chin)	—	—	—	—	75/ - / - /45
Lateral Bending (bring ear close to shoulder)	—	—	—	—	45/ - / - /45
Rotation (turn head to right and left)	—	—	—	—	80/ - / - /80

SHOULDER	1	2	3	4	5
Abduction (bring arm up sideways)	0 - 90	—	—	0 - 90	180/170/ 180/180
Adduction (bring arm towards midline of body)	90 - 0	—	—	90 - 0	50/ - / - / -
Vertical (forward) Flexion (raise arm straight forwards)	0 - 90	158	166.7 (+ or - 4.7)	0 - 180	180/170/ 130/180
Vertical (backward) Extension (raise arm straight backwards)	0 - 50	53	62.3 (+ or - 9.5)	0 - 50	50/30/ 80/60
Horizontal Flexion (while prone, raise arm towards chest)	—	135	140.7 (+ or - 5.9)	—	- / - / - / 135
Horizontal Extension (while prone, lower arm towards back)	—	—	45.4 (+ or - .2)	—	- / - / - /45
Internal (medial) Rotation	0 - 90	70	68.8 (+ or - 4.6)	0 - 90	90/90/70/ 60-90
External (lateral) Rotation	0 - 90	90	103.7 (+ or - 8.5)	0 - 90	90/90/70/ 90

ELBOW	1	2	3	4	5
Flexion (bring lower arm to biceps)	0 - 160	146	142.9 (+ or - 5.)	0 - 160	140/145/ 145/145

ELBOW	1	2	3	4	5
Extension (straighten out lower arm)	15 - 0	0	0.6 (+ or - 3.1)	145 - 0	0/0/0/ 0 -10

FOREARM	1	2	3	4	5
Pronation (turn lower arm so palm of hand faces down)	0 - 90	71	75.8 (+ or - 5.1)	0 - 90	80/90/90/80
Supination (turn lower arm so palm of hand faces up)	0 - 90	84	82.1 (+ or - 3.8)	0 - 90	80/85/90/90

WRIST	1	2	3	4	5
Flexion (palmar) (bend wrist so palm nears lower arm)	0 - 90	73	76.4 (+ or - 6.3)	0 - 90	60/90/ - /60
Extension (dorsiflexion) (bend wrist to opposite direction)	0 - 70	71	74.9 (+ or - 6.4)	0 - 70	60/70/70/50
Abduction (radial deviation) (bend wrist so thumb nears radius)	0 - 25	19	21.5 (+ or - 4.0)	0 - 25	20/20/20/20
Adduction (ulnar deviation) (bend wrist so pinky finger nears ulna)	0 - 65	33	36.0 (+ or - 3.8)	0 - 65	30/30/35/30

METACARPOPHALANGEAL JOINT (MCP) (fingers only)	1	2	3	4	5
Flexion	0 - 90	—	—	0 - 90	—
Extension	0 - 30	—	—	0 - 30	—
Abduction	0 - 25	—	—	0 - 25	—
Adduction	20 - 0	—	—	20 - 0	—

PROXIMAL INTERPHALANGEAL JOINT (fingers only)	1	2	3	4	5
Flexion	0 - 120	—	—	0 - 120	—
Extension	120 - 0	—	—	120 - 0	—

DISTAL INTERPHALANGEAL JOINT (fingers only)	1	2	3	4	5
Flexion	0 - 80	—	—	0 - 80	—
Extension	80 - 0	—	—	80 - 0	—

METACARPOPHALANGEAL JOINT (thumb only)	1	2	3	4	5
Flexion	0 - 70	—	—	0 - 70	—
Extension	60 - 0	—	—	60 - 0	—
Abduction	0 - 50	—	—	0 - 50	—
Adduction	40 - 0	—	—	40 - 0	—

INTERPHALANGEAL JOINT (thumb only)	1	2	3	4	5
Flexion	0 - 90	—	—	0 - 90	—
Extension	90 - 0	—	—	90 - 0	—

BACK (Lumbar)	1	2	3	4	5
Flexion	—	—	—	—	45-50/ - / - /45
Extension	—	—	—	—	25/ - / - /20-35
Flexion/Extension (sagittal)	—	—	—	—	—
Right Lateral Flexion	—	—	—	—	25/ - / - / 30
Left Lateral Flexion	—	—	—	—	—
Lateral Flexion (coronal)	—	—	—	—	—
Right Axial Rotation	—	—	—	—	30/ - / - / 45
Left Axial Rotation	—	—	—	—	—
Axial Rotation (transverse)	—	—	—	—	—
Lordosis	—	—	—	—	—

HIP	1	2	3	4	5
Flexion (flex knee and bring thigh closer to abdomen)	0 - 125	113	122.3 (+ or - 6.1)	0 - 125	100/120/ 125/120

HIP	1	2	3	4	5
Extension (move thigh backward without moving pelvis)	115 - 0	28	9.8 (+ or - 6.8)	115 - 0	30/10/10/30
Abduction (swing thigh away from midline)	0 - 45	48	45.9 (+ or - 9.3)	0 - 45	40/45/45/45
Adduction (bring thigh towards and across midline)	45 - 0	31	26.9 (+ or - 4.1)	45 - 0	20/- /10/ 0 - 25
Internal (medial) Rotation (flex knee and swing lower leg towards midline)	0 - 45	45	47.3 (+ or - 6.0)	0 - 45	40/35/45/ 40 - 45
External (lateral) Rotation (flex knee and swing lower leg away from midline)	0 - 45	45	47.2 (+ or - 6.3)	0 - 45	50/45/45/45

KNEE	1	2	3	4	5
Flexion	0 - 135	134	142.5 (+ or - 5.4)	0 - 130	150/120/ 140/130
Extension (hyperextension)	120 - 0	—	—	120 - 0	—
Lateral Rotation (twist lower leg towards midline)	—	—	—	—	—

ANKLE	1	2	3	4	5
Plantar Flexion (move foot down)	0 - 50	48	56.2 (+ r - 6.1)	0 - 50	20/45/45/50
Dorsiflexion (move foot up)	0 - 20	18	12.6 (+ or - 4.4)	0 - 20	30/15/20/20
Pronation (turn foot so sole faces in)	0 - 35	33	36.8 (+ or - 4.5)	0 - 35	—
Supination (turn foot so sole faces out)	0 - 25	18	20.7 (+ or - 5.0)	0 - 25	—

METATARSAO-PHALANGEAL JOINT	1	2	3	4	5
Flexion	0 - 30	—	—	0 30	—
Extension	0 - 80	—	—	0 - 80	—

INTERTARSO-PHALANGEAL JOINT	1	2	3	4	5
Flexion	0 - 50	—	—	0 - 50	—
Extension	50 - 0	—	—	50 - 0	—

References

1)   Physical Therapy: Merck Manual Professional, November 2005

2)   American Academy of Orthopaedic Surgeons: Average Ranges of Joint Motion

3)   Normal Range of Motion of Joints in Male Subjects: Donna C Boone BA RPT, Stanley P Azen PhD, The Journal of Bone and Joint Surgery Incorporated

4)   About.com: Sports Medicine, 16 July, reviewed by Medical Review Board

5)   Kinesiology: Scientific Basis of Human Motion: Luttgens & Hamilton, 1997 (from 4 sources)

Common Orthopaedic, Neurological and Other Tests

It is commonly the case that orthopaedic, neurological and other experts carry out tests, stating them to be positive or negative without explaining the significance of their results, or indeed what the test was intended to elicit. Hopefully, the following list will go some way towards filling the vacuum. A glossary of lesser-known terms, used in the descriptions below, appears at the end of the chapter.

ADAM'S SIGN [1]   A positive result is indication of a patient with a lateral curvature of the spine (scoliosis) which does not straighten on bending forward.

ADSON'S TEST [1]   The test is conducted to ascertain if a patient has a thoracic outlet syndrome (group of disorders involving compression at the superior thoracic outlet affecting the brachial plexus – a bundle of nerves that pass into the arm from the neck). The examiner palpates the radial pulse while moving the upper extremity in abduction, extension and external rotation. The patient is then asked to rotate his/her head toward the involved side while taking a deep breath and holding it. A positive exam will result in a diminished or absent radial pulse.

ANTERIOR DRAWER [2]   A test to ascertain a tear of the anterior cruciate ligament (knee), signified by excessive movement of the tibia.

APLEY TEST [1]   To determine the presence of a meniscal tear (knee). If lower leg rotation during compression of the knee elicits pain, a tear is possible.

APPREHENSION TEST [4]   A test involving forceful abduction and external rotation of the shoulder which produces apprehension in patients with shoulder dislocation or subluxation (incomplete/ partial dislocation).

AXIAL COMPRESSION TEST [1]
A test under which pain elicited by pressing down on a patient's head may be indicative of pressure on the facet joints of the spine, narrowing of the neural foramen (space through which nerve roots exit the spinal canal to form peripheral nerves), and pressure on a nerve.

BABINSKI'S TEST [15] **(PLANTAR RESPONSE)**
The test involves scraping an object across the lateral sole of the foot from heel to little toe. Normally, the big toe will flex. If it extends and the other toes fan out, the test is positively indicative of upper motor involvement.

BRAINSTEM AUDITORY EVOKED RESPONSE (BAER) TEST [8]
A test using electrodes placed on the scalp and earlobes to diagnose hearing ability, which may indicate the presence of brain-stem tumours.

CAROTID DOPPLER STUDY (CD) [8]
This study involves the evaluation of the large blood vessels of the neck by ultrasound, looking for possible narrowing (stenosis).

CAROTID DUPLEX [3] **(Carotid Ultrasound)**
The use of ultrasound to detect plaque, blood clots or other problems with blood flow in the carotid arteries.

CEREBRAL ANGLOGRAPHY [8] **(Vertebral Angiogram Carotid Angiogram)**
Visualization of the blood vessels of neck, head and brain using X-rays. Procedure involves insertion of catheter into an artery, usually in the groin, which is advanced up to the neck. An inert dye is then injected, which can be seen on X-ray.

CHEST EXPANSION TEST [1]
An expansion of the chest less than one inch from maximal exhalation to maximal inspiration is indicative of arthritis; in particular, ankylosing spondylitis.

CLONUS TEST [1]
If upon dorsiflexion of the foot, the result is uncontrolled up and down motion of the ankle, the result indicates pressure on the spinal cord.

COMPUTED in **TOMOGRAPHY SCAN** [8] **(CT, CAT)**
A computer-assisted X-ray which two dimensional pictures are obtained of parts of the body.

DISCOGRAPHY [3]
A test to determine if intervertebral discs in the spinal column are a source of pain (since MRI and CT scans only illustrate anatomy but not the source of pain). The test involves inserting a needle into the space of the suspected

61

disc. A small amount of contrast dye is then injected, after which images are taken with a CT machine.

DOPPLER ULTRASOUND [3]

A test used to detect blood clots and blocked or narrowed blood vessels in almost any part of the body.

ELECTRO- MYOGRAPHY [8] **(EMG, Nerve Conduction Study (NCS))**

EMG and NCS study the function of individual nerves and muscles by measurement of nerve and muscle response to electrical stimulation and measurement of spontaneous muscle electrical activity.

ELECTROENCEPHA- LOGRAPHY [8] **(EEG)**

The measurement of the electrical activity of the brain elicited through electrodes placed on the scalp for the diagnosis and monitoring of seizures, epilepsy, sleeping disorders, encephalitis (inflammation of the brain), metabolic or chemical disturbances of the brain or recognition of large structural abnormalities (eg tumours).

ELY'S TEST [1]

If flexing the leg upon the thigh till the heel touches the buttock results in the pelvis rising off the table, the test is positive for inflammatory or traumatic lesions.

EVOKED POTENTIAL RESPONSES (EPR) [8]

Minute electrical signals generated by the brain and spinal cord when transmitting and processing responses to sensory stimuli, usually obscured by random electrical activity in the environment but which can be tested by taking numerous sequential responses (whether visual, auditory or somatorsensory) and averaging them out.

FINKELSTEIN'S TEST [2]

A positive result indicative of wrist tendonitis is produced when, with the thumb inside the palm, pain is produced on ulnar deviation of the wrist and hand.

GRAPHESTHESIA TEST [8]

Graphesthesia is the ability to recognize writing on skin purely by the sense of touch. Agraphesthesia suggests a lesion in the contralateral sensory cortex. The test in inapplicable unless primary sensation is intact bilaterally.

HOFFMAN'S SIGN [8]

A test for heightened finger flexor reflexes (akin to but not precisely equivalent to Babinski's test), elicited by holding middle finger loosely and flicking the fingernail downward, causing the finger to rebound slightly into extension. If the thumb flexes and adducts in response, Hoffman's sign is present, suggestive of an upper motor neuron lesion affecting the hands.

ILIAC COMPRESSION TEST [1]

If pain is elicited by pressing the iliac crests together, it is evidence of an intra-articular sacroiliac lesion.

INTRATHECAL CONTRAST ENHANCED CAT SCAN [3]

The procedure involves the removal of a small sample of spinal fluid by lumbar puncture. The sample is then mixed with a very low dose of intrathecal contrast dye and injected into the spinal sac. The patient is then asked to move to a position that allows the contrast fluid to flow to the area being studied. The dye merely enables the spinal canal and nerve roots to be visualized more clearly on a CT scan.

LACHMAN TEST [1,2]

A tear of the anterior cruciate ligament of the knee is indicated where there is excessive motion of the tibia anteriorly when pulled forward with the knee flexed at 20 degrees.

LASEGUE'S TEST [1,6] See Straight Leg Raising Test

LUMBAR PUNCTURE [8] **(LP)**

An insertion of a needle into the subarachnoid space (the space under the membrane surrounding the brain and spinal cord) of the lower lumbar region for diagnostic or therapeutic purposes by allowing access to the cerebrospinal fluid (CSF). Testing the CSF allows identification of, eg meningitis, encephalitis, multiple sclerosis, peripheral neuropathies and tumours.

MAGNETIC RESONANCE IMAGING (MRI) [8]

The use of powerful magnetic fields and radio waves to produce detailed images of body structures. Useful for soft tissues, brain, spinal cord, joints and abdomen. Magnetic resonance angiography (MRA) can be used to visualize isolated blood vessels.

McMURRAY'S TEST [1] The test involves the patient lying supine with knee fully flexed. The examiner then rotates the patient's foot outwards while slowly extending the knee. A painful 'click' indicates a tear of the medial meniscus (knee). Inward rotation of the foot

OCUCOPLETHSYS-MOGRAPHY [3] **(OPG)**

A test to detect the presence of blockage in the carotid arteries, by indirectly measuring blood flow in the ophthalmic artery, which branches from the carotid artery and supplies blood to the eye. If a pulse arrives at the ophthalmic arteries and earlobes at the same time it is usually indicative of the arteries being free of blockage.

PATELLAR APPREHENSION TEST [1]

Apprehension during slight knee flexion whilst pushing the kneecap laterally suggests patient has experienced a subluxation or dislocation of the patella.

PATRICK'S TEST (FABERE TEST) [1]

With the patient supine, knee is flexed and external malleolus placed over patella of the opposite leg, with pressure being exerted on the flexed knee. Pain is indicative of disease of the hip joint or lesions of the sacroiliac ligaments.

PHALEN'S SIGN [1,7]

Paraesthesias and pain from median nerve compression produced on flexion of wrist. Also known as carpal tunnel syndrome. A reverse manoeuvre involving hyperextension of the wrist also produces same symptoms.

POSITRON EMISSION TOMOGRAPHY (PET) SCAN [3]

A muclear diagnostic test to detect and stage most cancers. It can also provide early information about heart disease and many neurological disorders. The scan examines the body's chemistry and can map the biological function of an organ, detect suitable metabolic changes and may be used to determine if a tumour is benign or malignant.

POSTERIOR DRAWER [1,7]

A tear in the posterior cruciate ligament is indicated by excessive movement of the tibia when pushed posteriorly with the knee flexed at 90 degrees.

QUADRICEPS INHIBITION TEST [1]

Pain and grinding when pressure is applied over the superior aspect of the patella while the patient is asked to perform straight-leg raising indicates chondromalacia of the patella.

ROMBERG TEST [8]

The test involves asking the patient to stand with feet together and eyes closed (in order to remove three sensory systems which provide input to the cerebellum to maintain truncal stability). If the patient sways but returns to stability with eyes open, there may be a mild lesion in the vestibular or proprioception sensory systems. If there is instability even with eyes open the lesion may be more severe or may indicate midline cerebellar lesion. Instability may also be caused by lesion of the lower motor neurons or basal ganglia for which the patient must be subjected to different tests.

SELECTIVE NERVE ROOT BLOCK [3]

In this procedure a small needle is directed, using X-ray guidance, near the nerve being tested. A small amount of contrast dye is injected, which may increase the normal level of pain. If pain is reduced after the injection, the nerve is most likely causing the pain.

SHOUDLER IMPINGEMENT TEST (Neer Impingement Sign) [1,2]

If impingement is discerned during forceful abduction or adduction and internal notation of the shoulder causing the greater tuberosity to press against the undersurface of the acromion, the test is positive.

SINGLE PHOTON EMISSION COMPUTED TOMOGRAPHY (SPECT) SCAN [3]

A nuclear test that provides information about blood flow to tissues and metabolic activities in the body; to identify areas in the brain involved in producing seizures in epileptic patients, to identify certain types of tumours and infections.

SLOCUM TEST [1]

A test to ascertain rotatory instability of the knee by rotating the foot internally and externally with the knee flexed at 90 degrees.

SOMATOSENSORY EVOKED RESPONSE (SSER) TEST [3]

A test for the detection of problems with nerve fibres that transmit sensation from the body to the brain as they travel through the spinal cord, brainstem and cortex.

STEREOGNOSIS TEST [8]

Stereognosis is the ability to perceive the form of an object by the sense of touch. Astereognosis suggests a lesion in the contralateral sensory cortex. The test is inapplicable unless primary sensation is intact bilaterally.

STRAIGHT LEG RAISING TEST (SLR) [1,6]

With the patient supine or seated and the knee extended, the hip is flexed (with the leg straight). Pain is suggestive of disc herniation, affecting the sciatic nerve distribution, and lumbo-sacral nerve-root compression.

SUPRASPINATUS ISOLATION [1] A test for a tear of the rotator cuff (shoulder) involving abducting and forward flexing with the forearm in internal rotation and looking for weakness.

TENSILON TESTING [8] A diagnostic test involving intravenous injection of the chemical edrophonium (tensilon) used specifically to aid in the diagnosis of Myasthenia Gravis, a disease in which there is a problem with the communication between the nerves and muscles.

TINEL'S SIGN [1] Percussion over the site of a divided nerve producing tingling sensation in the distal end of a limb indicates a partial lesion of the nerve or the beginnings of its regeneration.

TRENDELENBURG TEST [1] Patient is asked to stand on one leg, then the other. Where there is gluteus medius weakness on one side or a dislocated hip, the pelvis on the healthy side falls instead of rising when patient stands on affected limb.

WADDELL TEST [1] A test suggestive of functional overlay in patients with back problems, when patient tested for appropriateness of response to tenderness on axial loading, rotation, SLR in the seated position and overreaction. Inappropriate responses in 3 out of 5 areas suggestive of overlay.

Glossary of Terms

Acromion The projection of the scapula (shoulder blade) that forms the point of the shoulder.

Ankylosing Spondylitis A chronic inflammatory arthritis affecting joints in the spine and pelvis, which can cause eventual fusion of the spine.

Chondromalacia Pain at the front of the knee from almost any cause.

Greater Tuberosity That part of the humerus situated lateral to the head of the humerus.

Meniscus A C-shape piece of fibrocartilage located at the peripheral aspect of the knee joint.

Neuropathy Disorder of the nerves of the peripheral nervous system, although, according to some sources, it includes a disorder of the cranial nerves.

Proprioception The sense of the relative position of neighbouring parts of the body,

[1] Stanley Consulting, I Scoliosis
[2] Wheeless Textbook of Orthopaedics
[3] Neurosurgery Today: American Association of Neurological Surgeons
[4] American Academy of Family Physicians
[5] Medicine Net
[6] Spine Universe
[7] WebMD
[8] Neuroanatomy Through Clinical Cases, Hal Blumenfeld, MD, PhD